OUTDOOR STYLE

PENNY SWIFT · JANEK SZYMANOWSKI

OUTDOOR STYLE

STRUIK

Struik Publishers (Pty) Ltd
(a member of The Struik Publishing Group (Pty) Ltd)
Cornelis Struik House
80 McKenzie Street
Cape Town 8001

Reg. No.: 54/00965/07

First published in 1993

Editor: Peter Joyce
Editorial assistant: Glynne Williamson
Designer: Janice Evans
Assistant designer: Lellyn Creamer
Layout artist: Clarence Clarke

Typesetting by Diatype Setting CC, Cape Town
Reproduction by Unifoto (Pty) Ltd, Cape Town
Printed and bound by South China Printing Co. Ltd., Hong Kong

ISBN 1 86825 237 X

CONTENTS

ACKNOWLEDGEMENTS

When a book of this kind is conceived, very few of us imagine how many people will be involved. Not only does it take months of intense research and writing, and of travelling far and wide to photograph locations, it also takes a whole team to make the project a reality.

We thank them all, especially those with whom we were directly involved for so many months, in particular designer Janice Evans and design assistant Lellyn Creamer, editor Peter Joyce and project co-ordinator Glynne Williamson.

Then there are those who contributed advice and encouragement. Our sincere thanks to the experts who read the manuscript or sections of the text to ensure its accuracy. In particular, landscape architect Ian Ford of Ian Ford and Associates, who concentrated on aspects of style; Herbie Nash of Blue Mountains Nursery in Constantia, who made horticultural suggestions; and Gwen Fagan, an authority on the Cape Dutch genre.

Many people suggested locations, even if their own gardens were not suitable. It is not possible to list everyone, and we apologise to those not mentioned by name. There are also those who prefer to remain anonymous: they know who they are, and we thank them most sincerely.

Several people connected with companies also pointed us in the right direction. In particular we are grateful to Doug Lawson of Bolt-on Windows in Johannesburg, who makes splendid gazebos and conservatories; Peter Oudhof of Clearwater Pools in Pretoria; Roger Cluer of South Pools and Mike Cluer of Beach Pools, both operating in the Cape Town area; and Errol Cooper of Valley Tropical in Hout Bay.

Most of the landscapers and landscape architects whose work is reflected on these pages are acknowledged alongside the illustration.

Perhaps the most difficult task was finding suitable examples to illustrate Part One. Whilst many gardens are featured in this section, we offer special thanks to architect David Morrison, whose Italianate garden at Villa d'Este in Johannesburg perfectly portrays the European style; architect Francois Pienaar and his wife Serita, who have established a Japanese-style garden in Johannesburg, and which we have featured prominently; Lorraine Kettley, whose garden at Rosehurst in Pietermaritzburg illustrates the Victorian genre so beautifully; and Hope Beaumont, who, inspired by some of the world's greatest gardeners, has created wonderful English Country and Cottage gardens on her family farm, Valley Green, Elgin, in the Cape Province.

In addition to those professionals mentioned elsewhere on this page, a number of architects' gardens and outdoor features appear. We are grateful to all of them for their assistance: Carmel Back and Gerald Gordon of Johannesburg; Jannie Laubscher and Peter Loebenberg of Cape Town; and John Rushmere of Port Elizabeth. We also thank several interior designers and decorators, whose talents extend beyond the exterior walls of their houses; in particular, Daan Erasmus and Henri Pretorius of Johannesburg; and Marina Niven of Port Elizabeth.

Several official residences and properties in Cape Town are also featured, including the parterres at Tuynhuys, the gardens at Groote Schuur, Leeuwenhof and Bishopscourt, the Dolphin Pool at The Castle, as well as the front garden at Melrose House, now a museum.

We also thank Anglo American Farms for letting us include the gardens at Vergelegen in Somerset West; and Professor Robert Charlton and his wife Margaret for giving us access to their home Savernake, the residence of the vice-chancellor of the University of the Witwatersrand.

A big thank you, too, to Barbara and Peter Knox-Shaw who so graciously allowed us to photograph the gardens at Freshwoods, which were created by Peter's mother, the late Maisie Knox-Shaw; and Joan Brickhill who without a second thought, agreed to us photographing her lovely property at short notice (little more than an hour before she was due to leave South Africa to visit America).

Others who so generously allowed us to invade their privacy were Willie Barlow, whose garden at Birch Hill in Johannesburg is one of the most beautiful in the country; Barbara Hey, whose charming garden at Herb House in Wynberg, Cape Town, is always a pleasure to photograph; and Jackie Ravenscroft, owner of Spes Bona herb farm in Hout Bay and an inspiration when it comes to this subject.

Also, Malcolm Adamson; Barbara Alexandru; Sharon and Ian Armour; Terry and Carol Barnes; John and Lorna Barry; Gerhard and Kim Batha; Margot Berzack; Eugene and Liz Bester; Piet and Helen Beukes; Bill and Irene Clarke-Grey; Mike and Jean Collins; Errol and Helen Cooper; Gim Christie; Pat and Penny Cronin; Douglas and Lorraine de Jager; Gerrie and Ingrid Dekker; Di and Kim Dunbar; Joke Glauser; Diane and Henry Hall; Tim and Nick Hancock; Jannie Haremse; Jenny Haytread; Jan Hemmes; Marie and Fred Kolsch; Lee and Steve Leith; Peter and Peggy Loebenberg; Zan Louw and Willi Howell; Tony and Carol Mansfield; Esti Mellet-Mass; Marina and Patrick Niven; Ludwig and Sue Paulus; Jack and Di Penn; Christopher Peter; Stephanie Richards; Barbara Robertson; Kay and Steve Shapiro; Bill, Jill and John Smith; Dawn and Peter Smorenburg; Pepe Sofianos and Don Watson; Yvonne Stayne; Greta and Gino Stefanutti; Cobus Stofberg and Heber van Zyl; Gill and Simon Susman; Colleen van den Abele; Anke and Leon van der Walt; Danie and Erica van Loggerenberg; Henk and Anita van't Hof; Maureen and Henri Viljoen; Ruth and Terry Weldon; and Suzanne and Jan Wilmering.

An extra-special thank you to Gail and Jochim Bushel, whose stunning swimming pool, deck and outdoor entertainment area appear on the front cover; and to Jenny Larken, whose outdoor entertainment area is featured on the back.

INTRODUCTION

The creation and tending of gardens is one of man's oldest occupations. Even the most ancient of urban civilizations featured gardens, surviving pictures of which show us that they were sometimes functional, maintained to provide food; sometimes sacred (and, in hot climates, usually well shaded for practical reasons), or simply beautiful, contrived exclusively to give pleasure. Some of the latter, among them the legendary Hanging Gardens of Babylon and those created for the Roman Emperor Hadrian at his villa at what is now Tivoli, were quite remarkable.

Though Medieval cloister gardens were created essentially for prayer and contemplation, the general emphasis in that period was on the practical approach, with kitchen gardens, ornamental orchards and infirmary gardens full of medicinal herbs predominating.

Today there is a vast diversity of garden types and styles: some are strictly formal, others informal; some are based on traditional examples of various genre. However, most are simply practical, multi-purpose designs that make the most of a limited space.

Over the years a huge amount has been recorded and written, both locally and internationally, about gardens and garden making, indicating an intense interest in the subject throughout the world. This preoccupation is not surprising since there are few people who do not yearn to live in beautiful surroundings, to savour the fragrances of nature, and to enjoy the charm or splendour of a well planned outdoor area.

You may envy those who have the ability to create lovely gardens for themselves, believing perhaps that you do not have the talent to make something similar. Or, conversely, you may have the confidence to take on the project, even if your knowledge is limited.

A narrow bridge crosses an attractive fish-pond. Imaginative planting introduces texture and pattern to the area.

OPPOSITE *An unusual waterway, created by Patrick Watson, spills across the brick paved driveway.*

Bear in mind that there are numerous excellent general and specialized gardening books on the market which offer guidance on layout and on the selection of suitable plants, and the photographs in these publications and in magazines will give you inspiration and a wealth of ideas. Garden clubs and associations are also a good source of information: most organize tours through established gardens, and their members will encourage and even give you some practical assistance. Commercial nurserymen, too, will generally be able to supply the basic facts you need to stock any outdoor area. They may not, however, have every species or variety of plant you want, nor the background knowledge about traditional garden styles.

The importance of a good basic design cannot be overemphasized, and if you have the budget you could hire a professional landscaper or garden company. With a sensible skeletal plan, you will be able to take over the actual planting as your confidence grows.

Whichever route you choose, give careful consideration to the size, shape and scale of plants as well as to the balance and proportion of the garden as a whole. To achieve overall harmony it is vital to ensure a consistent visual theme, one which may be linked to a certain style, prompted perhaps by the architecture of the house, or related simply to colour. Some people have the instinctive ability to gauge what is needed, others have to spend more time reading and assimilating what has been done elsewhere, drawing on the knowledge and experience of experts.

Garden design is a partnership between gardener and nature. Climatic and weather conditions, seasonal changes, the quality of the site and its soil, will all affect the scheme. So, too, will time: since plants are continually growing and dying away, the design will be in a constant state of change.

A garden takes years to become established. It also inevitably involves a certain amount of experimentation, of trial that leads to error — especially if one is working to a limited budget. But it is heartening to remember that many a great garden has had humble beginnings, growing gradually and improving and developing with time, drawing its success from inventiveness, imagination, patience and determination.

Whether you are planning a new garden, planting from scratch, or altering and expanding one that is already established, it is essential to have, from the outset, a clear idea of the result you are aiming at. If you are going to create a specific style or introduce a theme, ideas can be borrowed from photographs in books and magazines, and from other people's gardens. However, remember that your own needs and preferences are paramount. Decide whether your garden layout is to be formal or informal, and whether it is to be purely aesthetic, or functional enough to provide you and your family with food, herbs and cut flowers. If there are to be practical areas for entertainment and leisure, these must be incorporated during the planning stages.

Outdoor Style has been designed, with all this in mind, to serve as both an informative guide and an inspirational handbook. It does not aim at any particular income group or specific social group, and attempts to embrace the full spectrum of garden types and styles to give a wide range of possibilities for all garden makers.

The volume is divided into three parts, each dealing with a different aspect of the outdoor area. Every type of house (from country mansion to compact townhouse) is considered from all possible angles.

Part One, Planting in Style, profiles nine basic garden styles. Some of these — Cottage and Japanese, for example — are traditional, and are capable of being specifically defined; others are discussed in much broader terms to help those wishing simply to achieve a certain look.

Similarly, some of the locations featured are puristic, adhering rigidly to the requirements and limitations of a particular genre, while others are more flexible, sometimes even combining characteristics from several different styles in a single garden.

Relatively few of the period-garden designs we have featured were created during earlier times; Victorian and English Country gardens (see pages 37-43) are both gaining in popularity and some of those photographed were started as little as three years before. Others, though, are older and more established; while some, including several Cape Dutch examples, have been restored according to early descriptions.

Even though a garden should ideally reflect the architecture of the house, those we have chosen do not always do so. Which is understand-

OPPOSITE   A *striking entrance makes a witty statement.*

ABOVE   *The arched walkway leading to the front entrance of this house has a distinctly Mediterranean feel enhanced by the magnificent view beyond.*

ABOVE RIGHT   *A stylish colonnaded verandah draped to create a colonial effect.*

able enough: after all the owner of an ordinary modern suburban home will want to create an exterior environment that has character and style – a pretty garden with Victorian features, perhaps, or even a Japanese garden with raked sand and stark stones. Similarly, the owner of a typical Cape Dutch homestead (old or new) may quite validly prefer to cultivate an English Country impression rather than try and simulate the adapted look of the Netherlands.

Part Two, Design for Outdoor Living, is relevant to every exterior style – and to every garden, even if it bears no relationship to a specific genre. Here we look at all the practical aspects of outdoor design, highlighting specific options in terms of type and theme.

Although this is not strictly a 'how to' gardening book, this section does give basic guidelines for garden design as well as offer some practical advice. The need for a clearly defined planting plan is emphasized, together with the fundamentals of layout and plant choice.

Colour, which can transform any landscape however big or small, is discussed in detail, and illustrated with a selection of schemes ranging from the ever-popular all-white garden to that planted to give a brilliant show throughout the seasons.

We have tried to show that there are many variations when it comes to walling, screens and the garden floor. You will see, from the gardens featured, how different materials can be used with success. Sometimes the choice is suggested by a particular style, in other examples it was dictated by purely practical considerations, or simply by the wish to create a good-looking outdoor space. Included is a cross-section of locations to please most tastes.

Another aspect discussed in this part of the book is shelter – from the sun's harsh rays, to wind and rain. This does not mean that the approach here is entirely practical: on the contrary, we have tried to produce imaginative pictorial suggestions, which are a little different from the norm, along with the purely functional ones.

LEFT   *Colourful herbaceous borders laid out in the English Country style in the octagonal garden at Vergelegen, an historic, early 18th century Cape Dutch homestead. The gardens were restored recently by Ian Ford.*

ABOVE   *An informal pond set in a lawned garden, has been planted with ferns and bog-loving plants, including papyrus.*

OPPOSITE
LEFT   *A charming home built in imitation of the French Provencal style.*

RIGHT   *A circular pool with travertine surround is stunning in its simplicity.*

Part Three, the largest section of the book, is a visual exploration of the garden, a tour starting at the boundary of the property and ending at the front door. Here you will journey up driveways and down pathways and walkways, up and down steps, through gateways and arches; and imagine yourself relaxing on a variety of patios and timber decks, strolling along terraces or soaking up the sun in contained courtyards. Featured is a selection of structures – arbours, pergolas, gazebos, barbecues, carports and outbuildings – together with an assortment of seating types to suit both the formal and informal outdoor plans.

The tour continues through kitchen gardens (where a variety of vegetables and herbs are grown) and orchards, and then into water gardens graced by reflective ponds, trickling streams and splashing fountains both formal and informal. Here too you will find some of the swimming pools, hot water spas and various other areas for play and relaxation that have been incorporated into different garden plans.

Within the broad spectrum of sites and vistas appearing in this book you are likely to find much that appeals to you and which will work in your own particular situation. The gardens included were photographed in various areas, so climatic and regional variations are also represented.

The photographs that follow are intended to delight the eye, to stimulate the creative spirit, and to offer some practical assistance in the transformation of your outdoor living area. We hope that *Outdoor Style* will help give you confidence as well as ideas, and prompt you to tackle your garden with renewed enthusiasm.

PART·ONE

PLANTING IN STYLE

Garden design, like so much else, is subject to the dictates of fashion, changing according to the dynamics of taste and lifestyle. Gardeners also borrow freely from other times and other places, adopting and adapting distinctive styles – designs based on local climatic conditions, on custom, perhaps on philosophical and religious precepts – that have evolved in different eras and different parts of the world.

Part One, while not intended as a history of gardening, covers nine broad schemes, ranging from the period to the exotic, which have survived the passage of the centuries – and, some of them, the challenges of distance – to offer the contemporary gardener a wealth of ideas. An insight into the plantings, the colours, textures, structures and accessories traditional to these enduring genres will help you create that pleasing, characterful, very special environment.

The English Country style is suggested by a simple pedestal set in a circular clearing accessed by grass walkways and bordered by roses and various herbaceous plants.

Clipped cypresses are a fitting backdrop for classical statuary in the Italian style. Simple urns add to the look. Design: David Morrison.

OPPOSITE Pillars flank the entrance to the front garden of Villa d'Este. Although built on a much smaller scale, it incorporates the very essence of one of Italy's greatest Renaissance gardens, designed by Pirro Ligorio in the 16th century. Design: David Morrison.

EUROPEAN

This is essentially a classical look, formal, grand in both scale and imagination. Its origins can be traced to Ancient Rome, where villas incorporated formal courtyards, terraces and customary colonnades, cloisters and pool enclosures.

However, in modern terms, it derives its inspiration from geometrically laid out gardens of the kind made famous by the French and Italians during the Renaissance, designs that heralded a return to classical forms. The end result was larger than life — vast, magnificent, even pompous — but the qualities of balance and proportion remained all-important. Intricate parterres were so contrived that they could be seen from terraces and from the villa, palace, chateau or castle — as were potagers, the classic French kitchen gardens that were intended to be seen and admired rather than hidden from sight.

Topiary and monumental fountains (as well as a range of outrageous features, usually operated by water pressure) were also major elements, and with all this there was still room for garden follies.

Grottos, too, were a common feature — they may still be seen in Europe at the Villa d'Este in Tivoli, Villa Lante to the north of Rome, and the Boboli Gardens in the grounds of the Pitti Palace in Florence. The most incredible of these, perhaps, was that constructed at the Palace of Versailles, near Paris, which, before the grotto was dismantled, was encrusted with mirrors, mother-of-pearl, sparkling gemstones and coral.

Although there are differences between the French and Italian approaches, the similarities are even more apparent. In fact many of the great French gardens are based on the geometric design so beloved of the Italians but, because of the flatter natural landscape, the French designs generally lacked the beautifully ornate terraces which were so frequently constructed in Italy.

While few contemporary gardens are created in the genre, it is possible to achieve the look, even in a reasonably limited space. The many features found in these classical gardens are also relevant to formal gardens that are not strictly European in origin.

Colour and pattern

Surprisingly little colour is evident in this type of garden, the plantings largely restricted to foliage species, shrubs and trees. There is some colour in the parterre but this, too, is restrained and controlled. flowers are used with circumspection, only one type and hue planted within each box-edged bed.

However, there is often more colour in the potager: it might for instance include roses to add bright accents to the carefully arranged beds of ornamental vegetables and herbs.

The formal parterre (usually planted, but sometimes also created with water) was a favourite with both the Italians and the French. Box-edged beds with elaborate scrolls or coats-of-arms were created with the plants, though today the approach is seldom seen outside major public parks and gardens.

Plants

Since fine-clipped hedges and topiary (see pages 115-116) are features, plants such as box (*Buxus sempervirens*), yew (*Taxus baccata*), common myrtle (*Myrtus communis*) and the Japanese privet (*Ligustrum japonicum*) are common. Several herbs make attractive hedges, among them lavender (there are several *Lavandula* species, but both the hardy L. *angustifolia* or L. *spica officinalis* and half hardy L. *dentata* or L. *stoechas* may be used) and cotton lavender or santolina. Bay trees (*Laurus nobilis*) are suitable for simple topiary.

Infill planting for parterres should be kept simple, although here some colour may be introduced with perennials, including various primulas, pinks (*Dianthus chinensis*, D. *deltoides* and D. *plumarius* are all appropriate) or peonies (*Paeonia lactiflora* has poppy-like flowers and colours range from white and pink to red and purple), although these require a very cold climate to survive.

Among trees suitable for the framework of a European-style garden are the imposing deciduous common horse chestnut (*Aesculus hippocastanum*), attractive London plane (A. *x hispanica*), various maples, noted for their brilliant autumn foliage, and cherry trees (especially *Prunus avium* and the Japanese flowering cherry, P. *subhirtella*).

Flowers are used sparingly.

Generally, hard surfaces are more prominent nearer to the house itself, with softer plant material (including lawns) featuring further away.

Since parterres are so important to the European style, bedding plants must also be carefully considered. These may be combined with colourful gravels, brick dust, crushed coal, sand, or even marble dust.

Seating and structures

Structures aplenty, especially in specifically Italian-style gardens, where columns and lifesized statues – in niches or on plinths – feature, together with pavilions, belvederes, obelisks and decorative walls.

Wherever there is a change of level (on the larger property), the slope is dramatically exploited with exaggerated terraces, grand outdoor staircases, balustrades and pavements. Even courtyards can be created on a series of levels.

France, as we have noted, is a generally flatter country than Italy, so the typical French-style garden, if laid out in the traditional Renaissance manner, would contain these elements but lack the terracing. Treillage, an art developed in 18th-century France, is another typical feature (see page 204).

Movable benches in classic designs are common. These are often wooden, and may either be left unpainted or given a coat of white or perhaps a muted green paint.

Features and finishing touches

Many types of ornament and statuary – sundials, bird-baths, urns, cherubs – are appropriate. They should be suitably elaborate and large enough to attract attention: undersized features will do little to affirm the style.

Containers with clipped plants, including bay trees and box, may be used in courtyards or on formal patios. Classical and reasonably ornate pots are most appropriate, although white-painted timber boxes may also be incorporated.

Many Italian gardens sport lavish fountains and flourishes of water. Although few modern properties are suited to grottos of the sort constructed in the great Italian estates, smaller and more rustic caves remain typical of the genre.

ABOVE *In the forecourt of a 20th century Italianate property, architect David Morrison has combined brick pavers with slate to create typical geometric patterns.*

OPPOSITE *Lavender hedges, clipped cypresses, urns, statues, pillars and a classical sundial all contribute to the European genre. A row of Pride of India trees shield an informal herb and vegetable garden. Design: David Morrison.*

Surfaces and materials

Both grass and gravel walkways are found in gardens of the genre. The Italians, with their use of many types of beautiful marble, are the reputed masters of paving, so this material is an obvious choice for patios and terraces. Use bands and panels of different colours or textures to create rich and interesting patterns. Flagstones, too, are a suitable option and pebble mosaics may be incorporated.

Rocks, stones, pebbles and a hollowed-out water basin with floating flowers are complemented by a variety of plants, including bamboo and grasses.

OPPOSITE   *A koi pond introduces the symbolic elements of water and stone. Brown glazed pots add to the look of the Orient.*

ORIENTAL

The gardens of the Orient, and in particular those of old China, have been a source of inspiration to both eastern and western cultures for many centuries.

In diametric contrast to the early Egyptian gardens, which derived partly from the irrigated oases of a dry and sandy country, the early Chinese took their lead from grand Imperial hunting parks, all of them spacious and fertile landscapes of incredible beauty. Here there was a diversely rich selection of flora, with flowers, trees and shrubs of many species, to reflect the natural world (as opposed to the house itself which, according to the tenets of Confucianism, represented order in human life).

Various emperors have been credited with inaugurating the art in China. A 3rd-century ruler, dreaming of the legendary Mystic Isles, home of the Immortals, is said to have created a giant lake-and-island fantasia, with five-metre-high rocks to symbolize the isles. Over the centuries, the concept softened with gentler contours – but the basic approach remained unchanged: water and rocks (representing the yin and yang forces) were still the most important elements, followed by architecture, and only then by flowers, shrubs and trees.

Although the Oriental approach is essentially a natural one – and, like the great gardens of the Landscape Movement in Britain (see page 203), frequently incorporates 'borrowed views' of surrounding fields or hills – outdoor spaces are divided into a series of courtyards or enclosures and are not planned to be seen in a single sweep of the eye. Paths, fences and walls are never straight (evil influences are thought to travel a direct route), thus adding to the impression of an ever-changing landscape.

There is, of course, a similarity between Japanese gardens (see pages 25-27) and those found in other parts of the Eastern world. Although the land formations of Japan are entirely different from those of China, the Japanese assimilated much of the Chinese culture. The Japanese, though, place emphasis on simplicity, rusticity, on the search for perfect harmony, while the Chinese approach is generally less formal and a lot more colourful.

There is a wealth of symbolism in the gardens of both countries. But the western mind finds it difficult to grasp the intricate meanings implicit in Oriental religious and secular philosophies, so beware of creating something that looks wholly contrived.

Colour

The Chinese, as mentioned, tend to have more flamboyance than the Japanese. There is a naturalness of colour in the gardens of the former, although these sometimes have bold highlights. Red is of prime importance; rich blues and greens may also be used to advantage.

Plants

The number and variety of these is limited, and those that are featured invariably have symbolic relevance. The sacred lotus (*Nelumbo nucifera*) that sways above a garden pond represents the Buddhist soul rising, and is a token of purity and perfection; the chrysanthemum that flowers late in the year (and is, interestingly, Japan's national flower) embodies resilience and longevity; the flowering plum (*Prunus salicina*), which blossoms early, means hope and courage; bamboo (of which there are many different types) bends with the wind but does not break, so indicating dependability and honour. The sturdy pine is a symbol of august age and respectability; the peach promises fruitfulness and immortality; peonies (and the tree peony, *Paenia suffruticosa*, in particular) wealth and elevation in rank, and orchids, the human quality of grace.

Surfaces

Both water and stone, which, as we have seen, are symbolic, are vital elements; rockeries and streams or ponds are the order of the day. The Chinese also have a passion for displaying single stones, chosen carefully for their shape and form.

There is a focus on things natural; patio and terrace floors are tiled or paved, or laid with pebbles set into concrete, preferably to form a pattern. Timber decking may also be incorporated.

Although gravel is suitable as a surface covering, the Japanese-style sand garden is entirely inappropriate.

OPPOSITE Pebbles and bamboo — which represents honour and dependability — encircle a Japanese lantern in the corner of a courtyard garden. Design: Mary Jackson.

ABOVE A glazed Chinese pot, Japanese lantern and single bonsai tree are placed on either side of a stepping stone path.

ABOVE RIGHT A charming, little koi pond with obvious Oriental overtones.

Structures

Those included are architecturally distinctive. A pavilion, for instance, will feature brightly coloured fretwork and perhaps latticed sides; bridges are arched (the original design allowed sailing boats to pass beneath) and commonly lacquered in deep red.

'Spirit walls' of bricks and mortar were traditionally built inside the courtyard to screen the interior of the house and deflect evil spirits. Meandering garden walls are designed for peacefulness. A favourite feature, built into these structures, is the moon gate, a circular opening that symbolizes heaven.

Features and finishing touches

Lovely glazed pots, often green or brown in colour, are common in Chinese gardens. Many display the traditional dragon design.

Among other simple ideas that add to the look are well-sealed wooden barrels or attractive glazed ceramic pots, which may serve as miniature ponds. Add a couple of water lilies and a few small fish, and you will have created a good-looking feature which is highly original.

Avoid a look that is either too simple or, conversely, too cluttered with Eastern-style ornaments.

A neatly raked sand garden, with bamboo growing along the boundary.

OPPOSITE   *Rocks and stones have been meticulously placed for maximum effect in this sand garden. The grouping on the right suggests a turtle, a symbol of longevity. The carefully raked sand represents the waves of the sea or a lake.*

JAPANESE

The Japanese have developed the art of gardening to the point of exquisite perfection with their delicate arrangements of water, rocks, stone and sand.

Several distinctively different Japanese garden types have evolved over the centuries, including the traditional Zen Buddhist garden with its raked gravel; the classical stroll garden that features lakes, bridges and natural scenery; and the tea garden, set in a secluded corner and surrounded by a bamboo fence or hedge for privacy.

Most residential stands in modern Japan are tiny, of course, but the classical gardens of three to five hundred years ago were created on huge Imperial properties. On the other hand the temple gardens of the Zen Buddhist monks (who were devotees of the tea ceremony) were of a more modest size, while the tea garden itself was fairly small.

While the tea garden is probably the easiest style to emulate, much of what goes into a contemporary Japanese garden design derives from the meditative Zen Buddhist sand-and-stone arrangement (intended to be viewed rather than used). An essential aim here is to reproduce the idea of a natural landscape – a few large rocks around the base of a mound may suggest a mountain; a group of small trees a forest; an irregular, winding stepping stone path across open gravel the difficult route through life.

The overall design is asymmetrical; whilst overlaying the whole is an air of serenity and simplicity, even frugality.

Space is a prime element; perspective is subtly contrived: a large tree planted near the house and smaller ones on the boundary will give the illusion that the the latter are farther away, thus visually enlarging the garden. A partially obscured view will reinforce the effect and confer a touch of mystery.

The Japanese value the tranquillity of water and often incorporate ponds (and, on the larger properties, even a small lake) close to the house. The still surface reflects the images of trees, shrubs and, at night, the moon. Water also introduces movement and sound – with the trickle of a cascade or a gentle swish as koi break the surface of the pool.

Layout

An authentic Japanese-style garden will be an uncluttered place of clipped shrubs (often in traditional rounded shapes), stepping stones over water, stone lanterns, raked sand or gravel and an imaginative use of rocks and stones.

Larger properties are often divided into a series of smaller 'gardens'. Here, bamboo screens, open trelliswork and shrubs all have an important role to play.

If you have the space, consider creating a traditional tea garden in place of an entertainment patio.

Colour

Subtle colour is a vital element in the Japanese-styled garden. Light-toned neutrals are integral to both the inside and outside of the house. Avoid bold, garish hues. Aim for a delicate mélange of green shades combined with natural earthy colours: the browns, greys and terracotta.

Flowers do have their place, but they are more usually grouped near the house itself rather than used as part of the general landscape or to add colour to the overall scheme.

Surfaces and materials

Low-maintenance surfaces are a feature. White sand or gravel, either representing a dry river-bed or the sea, is usually raked with patterns in the Zen Buddhist style. Round stones and water-worn pebbles are placed around ponds or positioned as part of the imaginary river-bed. They should not be set in mortar or the natural effect will be lost. Rocks are usually grouped to evoke the idea of a rugged mountain or simply to symbolize the supreme qualities of strength and stability.

Stone or granite paths (including stepping stones) are a must. In the absence of the real thing, use simulated stone flagstones (made from concrete). The material may also be used for patios.

Moss is another typical feature. Encourage any type of moss (or ferns or a low-growing ground cover) to grow around rocks and stones and under trees. If your area is too hot for moss, consider the many other ground covers before opting for a lawn – the Japanese seldom plant that type of grass.

Common materials used in the garden are timber (for decking) and bamboo (for fencing). Screens are prominent in the garden as well as within a house decorated in the genre. Use wooden and bamboo screens as partitions and backdrops.

Plants

'Architectural' plants are important; evergreen shrubs and trees provide the skeleton of the design. Avoid shrubs with large leaves; choose fine-leafed plants, and trees with asymmetrical shapes.

In most gardens in Japan, trees and shrubs are severely pruned to bring them into proportion with the space available. (On the larger property it is usually only the rugged black pine trees that are pruned.)

Fine-leafed bamboo is perfect for planting along a boundary wall. Concrete paving stones add to the natural look.

There are many suitable arboreal species, but fruit trees that blossom in spring are irresistible. Consider japonica (*Chaenomeles japonica*) with its bright yellow, 'apple-blossom' flowers, or a flowering quince (*Chaenomeles speciosa*), which bears beautiful rosy-red flowers in spring.

For windbreaks, plant the hardy conifer, *Cryptomeria japonica* (Japanese cedar); and if you have a cool woodland setting, plant one or two Japanese maples (*Acer palmatum*), which are much admired in their motherland for the fiery hues of their autumn leaves.

No Japanese-style garden would be complete without bamboo. There are numerous species but, in general, it is the smaller ornamental varieties which are best suited to the average garden. The dwarf species, *Arundinaria auricoma*, has a lovely, stripy green-and-gold foliage, while sacred bamboo (*Nandina domestica*) has graceful, fern-like leaves.

Although Zen Buddhist gardens have no flowers, blooms and blossom play an important role in Japanese festivities and traditions. Evergreen camellias (*C. japonica*) and azaleas (*Rhododendrons*), both of which are indigenous to Japan, will provide glorious colour in spring and early summer, and a timeless quality throughout the rest of the year. Several perennials and bulbs are grown to perfection in Japan, including the Japanese anemone (A. *japonica*) with its rosy-purple, pink or white blooms. A few flowers are acceptable, including the chrysanthemum, the national flower of Japan.

While bonsai is not part of the garden itself, you can add to the Japanese feel by grouping a few favourite dwarf trees in sheltered corners of the patio or on a verandah.

Lighting

Perhaps the most valued source of light in a Japanese-style garden is the moon. An authentic garden features trees with branches arranged (usually with the aid of wooden poles set in the ground) to allow moonlight to shine through.

Stone lanterns (concrete imitations are widely available; metal and wood are suitable alternative materials) are an essential accessory. In use since the 17th century, they are often partially concealed by foliage, and may serve to light entrances and pathways or to draw attention to particular features. Lanterns were traditionally lit by placing a bowl of oil with a floating wick inside, though nowadays candles are more often used.

Lantern styles differ, but most are modelled on those found in old temples.

Features and finishing touches

Ornamentation is kept to a minimum. Lanterns are traditional; rocks and stones, as mentioned, serve as symbolic features; and water basins, set in beds of gravel or pebbles, can enhance the look.

Round stones have been used to create an imaginary 'river of life' in a woodland setting where Japanese mondo grass is an effective ground cover. Design: Patrick Watson.

The ultimate finishing touch here is a slave bell hung in the Cape Dutch style. This traditional bell-arch was constructed in about 1975.

OPPOSITE *A traditional holbol gable adorns the front facade of a 17th-century Cape Dutch home. The tiled verandah is covered by the roof structure of the thatched house, giving shelter to those wishing to sit outdoors. A crudely fashioned sundial in the garden bears various inscriptions, including the date 1756.*

CAPE DUTCH

Cape Dutch is a well-known and uniquely South African style of architecture. It is not, however, as well defined as an *outdoor* idiom, as few (if any) original gardens survive. In fact many of those created in the grounds of celebrated Cape Dutch properties have 20th-century antecedents.

It is likely that most of the original Cape Dutch gardens were styled along the lines of those in the Netherlands, the homeland of a large percentage of the settlers who inhabited the south-western Cape of South Africa during the 17th and 18th centuries. These were, in many ways, typically European in character (see pages 17-19); formal, symmetrical, with arbours, hedged walks and parterres. They were not, however, as grand as those of aristocratic France and Italy, and because of the generally flat Dutch landscape they lacked many features typical of the era, including terraces and cascades. The canals of Holland, too, influenced the layout, as did the smaller size of the average Dutch property. There was also little emphasis on fountains and on the kind of waterworks

so popular elsewhere in Europe, probably because the local water pressure was not strong enough.

Moreover, the very earliest South African gardens were probably geared to subsistence living, with a focus on fruit and vegetables.

The most famous Cape Dutch example is the Dutch East India Company's garden in Cape Town established well over three centuries ago. Originally planned for an area of about 50 acres, it incorporated grazing land, vegetables, fruit trees, and a Baroque-style pleasure garden with aviary and menagerie (on the site of what is now Cape Town High School; the lion cage, though, was in the area now occupied by part of the University of Cape Town).

Research by author and historian Gwen Fagan (wife of the noted restoration architect, Gabriel Fagan) indicates a strong Dutch influence in the early Cape days, with formal beds planted in the European style – including square ones – and surrounded by hedges and planted with fruit trees, vegetables and ornamental species.

Although the boundaries of the Garden have shrunk over the centuries, some original features, including an imposing lily pond and formal herb garden, have been retained, as have some of the old plant specimens, among them oaks (planted from acorns brought from Europe), palms and magnolias.

The garden of Tuynhuys ('garden house'), built in 1682 by Governor Simon van der Stel as a guest house, is of course also a part of the original Company property. Restored by South Africa's Public Works Department in the 1960s according to a plan by G.T. Fagan Architects, it features formal parterres, hedges of clipped myrtle and rosemary.

More recently, yellow brick paving was laid in place of gravel paths for authenticity.

Plants

While many different flower varieties are incorporated in the modern Cape Dutch-style domestic garden, it appears that there were relatively few on the original properties. Of course, as time passed more and more species were introduced, and many have since become synonymous with the genre.

Most of the old homesteads feature oak-lined driveways that provide a backdrop to more recent plantings. Especially appropriate are citrus trees – in particular Seville oranges and Cape rough-skin lemons – planted in avenues.

Hydrangeas, originally imported from the Far East, are often seen along the front of the house and sometimes along a wide path leading to the front door. Grape vines and bougainvillaea are common over pergolas; both bay trees (*Laurus nobilis*) and myrtle (*Myrtus communis*) are suitable for topiary.

ABOVE *The formal parterres at Tuynhuys, originally laid out in the early 18th century, when Lord Charles Somerset was governor of the Cape in South Africa. They were restored about three decades ago.*

BELOW *The parterre garden at Tuynhuys in Cape Town, South Africa, features hedges of neatly clipped rosemary and myrtle.*

It was common practice to plant roses (which, for authenticity, should be of the old-fashioned type) in hedgerows, as well as myrtle and rosemary (*Rosmarinus officinalis*), clipped to form a framework for the formal parterres. In planting the parterres, it is especially important to choose species that will really thrive or the effect will be lost.

Perhaps ironically, indigenous flower species were not often seen in ordinary private gardens until the early 20th century, when the establishment of the world-famous National Botanic Garden at Kirstenbosch in South Africa stimulated an intense interest in these plants.

Surfaces

Most Cape Dutch houses feature a courtyard as well as the traditional stoep which is sometimes covered by a pergola or shaded by a tree or vines. The floor surfaces are often tiled with handmade Batavian or ordinary quarry tiles, for which both rough stone and clean-cut flagstones were often used. The contemporary patio, however, may be brick paved.

'Klompie' bricks, brought out as ballast in the Dutch East India Company ships, were often used for steps, edgings and trims around arches.

Although paths are sometimes stone or gravel, yellow brick paving is more correct.

Seating and structures

The traditional stoep may, but need not, have built-in seating at one end; nowadays, wooden benches and moveable furniture are more commonly used. However, most modern designs, and plastic in particular, should be avoided.

Sturdy, thickly plastered and whitewashed 'werf' walls are a feature around traditional homesteads. Ornate pillars may be positioned at the entrance but, since properties were usually large in size, simple pole fencing or hedges are often more appropriate for boundaries.

Rustic stone steps and chunky retaining walls (built from local stone or roughly plastered and painted white) are favoured where the ground slopes.

Features and finishing touches

The Dutch filled their outdoor spaces with lots and lots of pretty, fancy and above all colourful flowers, well-clipped hedges, formal parterres and topiary features. Fountains were seldom incorporated in their garden designs; statues were small in scale and often gilded or painted.

While immigrants to the Cape appear to have placed less emphasis on elaborate features than their compatriots who stayed behind (some researchers claim there were few parterres and no topiary), these touches are nevertheless in keeping with the genre. Wooden tubs or terracotta pots, thoughtfully planted along the front stoep and in the courtyard, will add welcome splashes of colour to the scene.

Formal ponds are usual in the gardens of the grander homes, either in front of the house or in the courtyard. And an old slave bell (or a copy) hung in a traditional arch, adds the ultimate finishing touch.

Ochre-washed walls flank the newly restored Dolphin Pool at the Castle in Cape Town, one of South Africa's most important national monuments.

A *grassy walkway meanders through a pretty Cottage-style garden planted with a selection of flowers and herbs including pink and yellow roses, scented geraniums, white valerian, cotton lavender, bright red Shirley poppies, pansies, yarrow, heliotropes, pink and purple* lychnis *and violets.*

OPPOSITE   A *slightly curved slate 'crazy paving' pathway leads family and friends to the front door of a modern cottage.*

COTTAGE

The Cottage garden is essentially informal, wholly unpretentious and always pretty in a picture-postcard kind of way. Walls are covered with climbers, and there is an abundance of fragrant and colourful flowers.

For all that, though, this is an essentially functional style. There are few empty spaces, very little lawn, and much that is useful within the glorious jumble of plants – fruit, vegetables and herbs for use in the kitchen and, to a lesser extent, flowers for picking and possibly sale.

Despite the apparently random mix of plants, though, there is some order to the arrangement, and to create a garden in the genre needs careful planning: only if close attention is paid to individual plants will the whole form a coherent and beautiful picture. One example here is the importance of establishing a selection of species that flower at different times of the year so it is never bare.

Pathways give shape to the Cottage garden. The main one (which should be about 1 metre or 3 ft wide) takes a reasonably direct route from gate to front door, while other, equally wide, secondary paths meander through the plantings in the garden.

The origins of the style can be traced to the homes of British cottagers who lived a largely subsistence peasant existence, depending on what they could grow for themselves. Plots were small, the planting fairly limited: there was little room for purely ornamental flowers (unless the landlord insisted on them), and those that were cultivated often had medicinal uses – honeysuckle leaves, for instance, were boiled to make a cough syrup; pansies were used to cure convulsions. Very few original Cottage gardens remain of course, and for inspiration we must rely on pictures and on contemporary designs created in the genre.

Victorian novelists and painters did much to portray and popularize the romantic notion of the Cottage garden. There were cottage gardening societies in Britain and a magazine, *The Cottage Gardener*, was devoted exclusively to the subject. And talented landscapers, including William Robinson and Gertrude Jekyll, drew inspiration from the concept.

The gardens they designed and planted, however, were on a grander scale and incorporated more features (see pages 41-43) than did the genuine article.

Contemporary Cottage gardens, though fairly faithfully reproducing the style, often omit the practical and functional aspects.

Layout

The garden plan depends on how the house is sited. If it is near the road, there is plenty of room for vegetables and fruit trees behind, and the entire front area can be filled with flowers. If, however, the dwelling is positioned towards the rear of the plot, fruit and vegetables will have to be accommodated in the front garden.

Vegetables are generally planted in neat rows, along with strawberries, gooseberries and so on, while a variety of herbs are often mixed with flowers near the kitchen door.

Colours and plants

An abundance of bright colours is the hallmark of this kind of garden, the cottagey effect achieved by planting a haphazard mix of flowers, fruits and herbs. Avoid modern species; concentrate on old garden plants (which, in addition to their visual suitability, are particularly hardy), especially on those that will self-seed, and on flowers that are indigenous to your area. Do not group these but, rather, plant a wide range of different species to form a haphazard, wild-looking riot of colour.

Some of the favourite Cottage plants include the hellebores (the Christmas rose, *Helleborus niger*, grows best in cool, moist regions), irises, rhododendrons, the heathers, clematis, forsythia (in particular golden bell, *F. suspensa*, a traditional Cottage garden plant), buttercups and daisies, peonies, periwinkles, primroses, snapdragons, pansies, cornflowers, tobacco plants, stocks, poppies, daffodils and tulips.

ABOVE LEFT *A narrow earth pathway winds through a pretty Cottage garden.*

ABOVE *The front door of a contemporary cottage is framed by brightly-hued bougainvillaea and Virginia creeper.*

OPPOSITE

RIGHT *A haphazard mix of flowers lines the approach to a country cottage. Wallflowers, roses and day lilies add colour to the scene, while a mix of tiny daisies and pennyroyal smother the rustic steps.*

FAR RIGHT *Herbs, shrubs and flowers combine to create a charming cottagey effect.*

Roses of course, are a must, especially the double or cabbage type, as well as other sweet smelling plants; jasmine (*Jasminum officinale* is the most popular), sweet peas, scented lilies, lavender, honeysuckle and wisteria.

Herbs, grown for their scent as well as for culinary and medicinal purposes, do not add much colour to the garden. However, mixed with the flowers, they enhance the look. Some commonly grown types are shrubs such as rosemary, lavender and sage; marjoram, fennel, basil, dill, angelica, chives and, close to the kitchen door, mint.

Typical fruits include apple, pear, plum and cherry trees, currants (red, black and white) and canes (including raspberries and strawberries). For authenticity, add a nut-bearing tree to the selection.

A traditional cottage may well have a wall built from local stone, but hedging is also common. Among suitable hedging plants are English hawthorn (*Crataegus oxyacantha*, which grows well in areas with a high summer rainfall), privet and yew.

Surfaces and materials
Natural materials abound in the Cottage garden. Ideally, pathways are made from local brick, stone, cobbles, laterite (see page 93) or even simply compacted earth or gravel, and fences (picket fences are a favourite) and gates are of wood. Metal gates – if indeed they feature – are simple in design and often left unpainted.

A water garden is not appropriate here (although a pond may be incorporated, especially if you want to keep ducks).

Seating and structures
Although structures are kept to a minimum here, arches and pergolas (see pages 100-101 and 151) are acceptable if smothered by creepers and climbers. They may be made of wood or metal, but must be simple in design for authenticity.

Any form of rustic seating is suitable in the garden. Ideally, position a wooden bench outside the front door or on the porch.

Other traditional structures which are acceptable in this type of garden include a dog kennel and, in country areas, beehives and pigsties.

Features and finishing touches
There are few distinctive man-made features in the cottage garden, and those that are incorporated tend to be simple and subtle. Statues, fountains and urns are taboo, but a bird-bath and bird-table are appropriate, decorative and, because they attract wildlife, functional too. A well was a common component of old, original Cottage gardens, but it must be a simple structure with an ordinary, no-nonsense winch mechanism.

Create an archway at the front gate, preferably by allowing the hedge to grow higher than the opening and then bending and training it over the top.

Container plants are often found alongside the house, in the porch and on windowsills. Since few cottagers could afford anything fancy, any kind of pot, bucket or barrel may be used.

The architecture and garden design of Melrose House in Pretoria, South Africa, is extravagantly decorative. Named after Melrose Abbey in Scotland, it boasts typically contrived features including a conservatory, gazebo and fish-pond.

OPPOSITE A small, formal white garden designed in the Victorian genre features an ornate bird-bath as its focal point. Old bricks have been used for the pathway, while old tiles edge beds and Victorian street lamps light up the garden at night.

VICTORIAN

Gardens created in what is perceived to be Victorian style are as fussy, cluttered and ostentatious as the interiors of the period. All inhibition is abandoned; while the choice of elements encompasses arbours, gazebos, sundials and lots of structures for growing plants up and over. Secret gardens, grottos, romantic seats and busy layouts based on carpets and tapestries are also in the genre.

The approach, moreover, is highly eclectic; features ranging from simple Japanese stepping stones to pretty Elizabethan knot gardens are all eminently appropriate (like the domestic interiors of the period, a wide variety of outdoor styles became fashionable at one time or another during Queen Victoria's 64-year-long reign).

However, although it is essentially the *mid-Victorian* interiors – those that were particularly fussily furnished and heavily draped – that we associate with the interior genre, it is the *early-Victorian* era that tends to inspire and influence the exterior style and basic garden planting.

In the early 1830s, following the landscape (or 'landskip') craze, British author and gardener John Loudon identified a 'gardenesque' arrangement, where the outdoor area was distinguishable from the natural landscape. The Victorians interpreted this to mean that it was valid to mix, not only exotic with indigenous plants, but the informal design with the formal.

Joseph Paxton, designer of the awesome glass-and-iron Crystal Palace which housed the Great Exhibition in London's Hyde Park in 1851, made the greenhouse an integral part of the Victorian garden. A gardener and engineer, he built many extensive structures for his employer, the Duke of Devonshire at Chatsworth, and for other clients.

On the more extravagant Victorian property, established annuals were taken from the greenhouse and planted in beds. Carpet bedding that imitated mosaic was wildly fashionable, and wealthy land-owners had the staff to enable them to change the plantings in just a few days. Although this horticultural art is now more commonly found in public parks, where motifs and crests are often reproduced, a generous flowerbed planted in this fashion will be sure to add authenticity to a contemporary garden in the style.

By the mid-Victorian period, the fussy approach had been challenged by several talented gardeners who advocated, among other things, generous herbaceous borders, meadows and wild gardens. The Irish-born William Robinson was a leading proponent, along with artist Gertrude Jekyll and the young architect Edwin Lutyens. While the style they popularized has Victorian overtones, it also produces a romantic elegance that deserves to be classed as a style in its own right (see pages 41-43).

Colour and pattern

Strong and varied colour – rather than form – is the essence, and the garden scheme may be either complementary or harmonious in theme (see pages 76 and 77). The Victorians had a mania for order and colour co-ordination, and so flowers are used to create carpet effects of different hues, often in a variety of distinctive patterns and designs.

Dwarf plants are generally used to create a mosaic or carpet bed. Where a taller plant is included in the plan, it is known as a 'dot' plant. Interestingly, it was the geranium (including pelargoniums and their garden hybrids) which Victorian gardeners considered *the* bedding plant.

Surfaces

Brick, grass and gravel paths are suitable, and patios may be of brick or timber. Encaustic tiles are typically Victorian, especially for porches and verandahs. If yours is not an authentic house, scrounge through demolition yards for discarded tiles, or simply paint a similar design.

A rockery is an appropriate inclusion, especially if it is planted with ferns and alpine plants. Use tiles to edge flowerbeds and keep gravel in place.

By all means incorporate a lawn – and breathe a sigh of relief that the lawnmower has improved in efficiency since Queen Victoria's day (it was patented by a Mr Budding in 1830). Or follow the example of the late-Victorians and plant yourself a wild meadow (see pages 72-73).

Plants and trees

Ideally, the garden should be filled with a mix of exotic plants, especially flowering species and ferns. Choose any type of flowerbed – round, raised or straight – but ensure there is a mass of colour.

For authenticity, include some species that were introduced to Britain during the reign of Queen Victoria: beautiful, easy-to-grow tiger lilies (*Lilium tigrinum*); enchanting Californian poppies (*Eschscholzia*) which mass so beautifully in a summer garden; deciduous *Kerria japonica* with blooms similar to the rambler rose; hardy *Buddleia davidii*; and colourful perennial Japanese anemones (*Anemone japonica*).

If you are planning a large shrubbery, consider *Forsythia suspensa* with its golden-yellow, bell-shaped flowers or the hardy deciduous, flowering Chinese wisteria (*W. sinensis*), which is a vigorous climber. For scent, be sure to include Chinese jasmine (*Jasminum polyanthum*), an easy-to-grow evergreen with pretty white to pinkish flowers.

Carpet bedding used to great effect in a small front garden. Several newly planted conifers have been clipped to form geometric shapes and the beginning of topiary birds and animals.

Even though formal features, including topiary hedges, and massed carpet bedding (sometimes planted in the patterns of heraldry or the shapes of animals) became less fashionable in the latter half of the 19th century, these are elements that will immediately identify your garden as Victorian.

A selection of evergreen conifers and a separate formal rose garden are a must.

Seating and structures

It is fairly easy to evoke the Victorian spirit by including in the general scheme a period-style gazebo, trelliswork, or even a more modern greenhouse (where you can propagate and tend plants that are not in peak condition), a modest verandah or simply a screened porch. Arches, tunnels and elaborate plant supports are also common. Although metal may be used, timber is the more favoured material for all these structures.

In addition, consider a custom-built garden seat that encircles a big shady tree, or place a variety of suitable benches (ideally, those designed in the period style) in secluded corners or wherever there is a pleasant view.

While furniture should be painted or varnished to prevent deterioration outdoors, Lloyd loom chairs (or even contemporary cane) are especially suitable for gazebos and verandahs. Elaborate cast-iron furniture is also popular.

Features and finishing touches

Fountains and statuary are the order of the day, with vases and shaped pots displayed on terraces. A sundial may be set in the centre of a formal herb or rose garden. Various designs modelled on those favoured by the Victorian are available, usually for mounting on a decorative column.

Carpet bedding creates a magical effect around a traditional sundial in the foreground. From here an old brick path leads through an arch to a charming, all-white garden complete with an inviting Victorian gazebo.

A *rustic stone bridge leads to a secret garden which typifies the Gertrude Jekyll concept of outdoor 'rooms'. A bench invites one to sit, while fruit trees and fragrant flowering plants attract birds and bees.*

OPPOSITE *Charmingly overgrown steps lead to a simple stone bench set amid fragrant roses in a typical English Country garden.*

ENGLISH COUNTRY

There is a timeless quality about the English Country garden that defies analysis. Definition is difficult, too, because, through the ages, great estates have been designed and have evolved in very different ways – some perhaps imitating the magnificent villas of Continental Europe, with their grand parterres, others following the teachings of the British garden designer Lancelot (Capability) Brown (see page 202), who replaced the formal styles of the pre-Victorian past with natural-looking landscapes.

Although its roots may lie in the late-Victorian era, English Country style in the contemporary sense involves a lot more than the passing fashions of a particular period. Rather, it embodies the essence of all that one associates with gracious living in a setting honoured by time. There is a well-loved, well-worn look about such an environment that matches the interiors of houses furnished and decorated in the genre. Surfaces have a patina of natural weathering; brick and stone walls are encrusted with moss and lichen; pathways are charmingly overgrown.

All this will take a long while to establish, but with care and patience it *can* be done. The approach is somewhat similar to that needed to create a really beautiful picture, one in which design, colour, texture and pattern contribute to the whole.

The Victorian artist, poet, socialist and Arts and Crafts campaigner William Morris was one of the most vehement critics of the middle-class fashions of that era. He especially loathed the habitual fussiness of his bourgeois contemporaries, and in his own garden he returned to a simple, romantic style that complemented his furniture and fabric designs. Traditional features included enclosed gardens, topiary and trellises, orchards, and simple cobbled paths; plants were of the old-fashioned kind, and beautiful.

It was, however, two of his contemporaries, the brilliant botanist and author William Robinson, and the artist, gardener and writer Gertrude Jekyll who, together with the younger architect Edwin Lutyens, probably did most to influence thinking in this field. Robinson shared the Arts and Crafts taste for simple, informal planting and, instead of seasonal carpet bedding, he advocated the use of permanent plants in deep borders along the sides of the property, and encouraged the incorporation of wild gardens. His magazine, *The Garden* (to which Miss Jekyll, inspired by the lovely informality of the stylized Cottage scheme, contributed), became a successful vehicle for their views.

In general, the style is best suited to rural spreads, especially those in areas which experience similar (though less severe) weather conditions to England – in Elgin in the south-western Cape of South Africa and parts of New Zealand's North Island, for instance. However, there is no reason why a city garden cannot be created in the genre, providing of course that there is space to accommodate it and the climate is moderate and not too dry.

Layout

The typical English Country garden, large though it may be, is divided into a number of smaller 'rooms' often around architectural features – an arrangement popularized by Gertrude Jekyll and Edwin Lutyens (who worked together from 1889), and one which provides variety and interest within the overall, stylistically coherent scheme. This enables one to plan a number of distinctive but complementary areas – for instance a formal swimming pool, a rock garden, a meadow (or the type of wild garden proposed by William Robinson), a rose garden, herb and vegetable garden *and* a water garden.

Inspiration may be drawn from many great English gardens, although probably the most internationally famous is Sissinghurst in Kent, the creation of amateur gardeners Vita Sackville-West and her husband, Harold Nicholson, who, like Jekyll and Lutyens, combined horticulture with architecture. Hidcote in Gloucestershire, laid out somewhat earlier (by another amateur, an American, Lawrence Johnston), is another fine example.

Miss Jekyll's own garden, at Munstead Wood, featured a formal terrace (with pots) leading to a lush green lawn and woodland beyond; and then there was a grey garden and the bold but well-composed borders she adored.

Colours and plants

Colour, a vital ingredient in the English Country garden, is displayed with confidence and aplomb, most typically, and prominently, by planting a substantial flower garden where sweeps of glorious colour can be seen from a distance.

Emulate Miss Jekyll (who, among other things, wrote the influential book *Colour Schemes for the Flower Garden*) and introduce generously proportioned herbaceous borders, ensuring that all the hues chosen are in harmony. Be inspired by her 'wonderful borders of graded colour' which lead you seductively through 'a static rainbow'.

ABOVE *A city garden laid out in the genre features several distinct areas including this formal rose garden incorporating a traditional grass walkway.*

OPPOSITE
RIGHT *A leafy pergola designed by Sir Herbert Baker at the turn of the 20th century.*

FAR RIGHT *Roses add colour and fragrance to the corner of a country garden inspired by Gertrude Jekyll.*

Colour schemes may be as simple or sophisticated as you wish. The English Country garden, however, is perfectly suited to the monochromatic approach (see page 77) featuring various tones of one particular hue, blue or gold for instance.

There is a vast number of appropriate border plants; among those especially recommended are hostas (*Hosta fortunei* is a good choice) and the hellebores (the Christmas rose, *Helleborus niger*, is perhaps the best known), peonies and lupins, although none of these are suited to hot, humid or very dry areas. Other possibilities are the hardy cranesbills (including *Geranium sanguineum*), salvias (especially S. *horminum* and S. *splendens*), various daisies, chrysanthemums, asters, delphiniums, larkspur and dahlias, day lilies (*Hemerocallis fulva*), phlox, irises and both tall and short campanulas.

Roses are, of course, an essential component. Well tended shrub roses make splendid informal hedges for country gardens but, better still, create a formal rose garden away from other flowers.

Seating and structures

Unless you prefer the Robinsonian approach and train creepers to grow over trees, a pergola is a must. However, this should, if at all possible, be constructed of local materials – provided, of course, they complement the architecture of the house. Use natural stone if it is readily available, or build the uprights of brick. Classical pillars are also appropriate in the right context. If concrete is used, it must be aged to provide the natural look.

The Lutyens and Jekyll pergolas, which supported creepers and climbers, provided an attractive link between house and garden. Cross-pieces were usually of timber, although similar structures sometimes featured wooden posts attractively joined together with chains or rope.

An arbour – which need not be as grand or as delicate as those created by Lutyens – is a typical feature of the English Country garden, as is a gazebo.

Benches and seats are made of wood and may be painted white, or distressed with a colour, or left unpainted and allowed to grow mellow with age.

Features and finishing touches

While some of the elements found in the Victorian garden (see pages 37-39) are appropriate, they are not featured with the same lavish indulgence. Among the possibilities are a sundial, a fountain, and pots on the terrace.

A *well-shaded seating area designed in true Mediterranean spirit. Fittingly, the fabric used to cover cushions was located by the owner, in Greece.*

OPPOSITE *Arches, a typical Mediterranean feature, add style to an outdoor area created in the genre. Furnishings and ceramics complement the look.*

MEDITERRANEAN

The Mediterranean-style garden evokes striking images of whitewashed walls brightened with cerise bougainvillaea and crimson geraniums in terracotta pots, courtyards and olive trees, tiled patios with trickling fountains, grape vines tumbling over pergolas and terraced slopes.

Typical examples can be found all over Spain, Portugal and Greece, and in France, where the visual dividing lines between interior and exterior are understandably blurred; where relaxed alfresco eating and a general simplicity of lifestyle are reflected in the overall outdoor and garden scheme.

Climates which are well suited to the Mediterranean approach are those found in the Caribbean, parts of California and South America, Australia and the North Island of New Zealand, as well as parts of South Africa.

The development of a Mediterranean style in fact has a lot to do with climatic conditions (and now allows for what we now commonly term 'indoor-outdoor living'). It also has cultural links, taking much from the gardens of the early Islamic Arabs – especially those of Moorish Spain. Here, a rectangular courtyard was a prime feature, an intimate and private oasis where trees gave dappled shade and water cooled the air.

This classical Mediterranean garden was formal, and the basic layout geometric, often with two main canals dividing the area into four (this symbolized the four Rivers of Life). Courtyards were walled or surrounded by a high hedge; paths were often raised so flower blossoms were level with the heads of those walking through the garden.

Water was also a common feature in the Moorish courtyards, and it remains so in the contemporary Mediterranean garden. It may take the form of a fountain, a simple trickle of water or a reflective pond.

A swimming pool may also be included in the garden plan, but it should be natural in character.

Drought rather than frost is generally the hazard in Mediterranean climes, so the type of plants traditionally featured are those that will thrive in hot, dry summers and mild, wet winters.

Colour

Natural colours – of the landscape or seascape – are the keynotes here. Stone or whitewashed walls form the backdrop for splashes of dirty green and brilliant blue, rusty ochre and dusky pink. Pink or red flowers are often displayed in earthy, red-brown terracotta pots.

Plants

Cacti, succulents and palms are common choices for the Mediterranean garden, although many other plants are suitable.

Pergolas – which are typical features – are often planted with grape vines or wisteria. Although not popular with domestic gardeners generally the Chinese gooseberry or kiwi fruit (*Actinidia chinensis*) is another possibility, but it is a tough, vigorous climber and needs a strong structure to support it.

Since many climbers will tend to have bare stems, you will have to plant shrubs around the perimeter to create the effect of shaded privacy.

Shade-giving trees are essential, of course, but they should be chosen with great care depending on the country and region. The Japanese pagoda tree (*Sophora japonica*), although slow growing, is a splendid shade tree; another, white stinkwood (*Celtis africana*) is suitable for the larger garden where available. Tall conifers are also a good idea, in particular the Mediterranean or Italian cypress (*Cupressus sempervirens*), which casts a long shadow.

Surfaces and materials

A lawn is not a feasible option in very dry Mediterranean areas; low-maintenance ground covers are planted instead (see page 93). Among the most

Terracotta roof tiles and exterior finishes give this southern hemisphere house an unmistakably Mediterranean look. Inspired by the traditional French Provencal style, it features walls rendered with coloured plaster and archways trimmed with cut stone.

popular species are easy-to-grow ivy (*Hedera canariensis*), periwinkle (*vinca major*), and *Ajuga reptans*. Gravel may be used for walkways, or to keep down weeds.

Patios and courtyards (and often other parts of the garden as well) are tiled with terracotta, quarry tiles or stone. Concrete may also be used, especially if set in places with cobbles or small river-stones. Brick paving is also common.

Verandah floors are often covered with matting of some sort, though ceramic tile decoration is also highly appropriate since it was a feature of both Moorish and Portuguese gardens.

Seating and structures
Structures are designed to create privacy and an air of seclusion, and to provide shade, and they include walls, screens, trelliswork, pergolas and pillars, all of which are used to support climbing plants.

Where terracing is a feature, traditional dry stone walls are the obvious choice. Here, too, permanent seating is often incorporated, and the effect softened with simple cushions and bolsters in traditional colours. Elsewhere wood, cane and metal are the most popular furniture materials.

Features and finishing touches
Pots of all shapes and sizes are a prominent element, largely because of the often dry summer conditions. Balconies, window sills, courtyards and patios are crammed with containers filled with flourishing, flowering plants, adding colour and charm to the exterior of the house and garden.

Choice of container is a personal matter, but terracotta pots – simple, earthy and unsophisticated – are integral to the patio or courtyard. Urns and vases will also enhance the look.

BELOW LEFT *A gum pole shelter adds to the character of an outdoor entertainment area with a distinctly Mediterranean feel.*

BELOW *Terracotta pots, planted with red geraniums, line stairways flanking the entrance to a courtyard.*

Geese meander near the front entrance of L'Ormarins, an historic dwelling built by Frenchman Pierre Joubert in the 19th century. Named after his Provencal home, La Morin, the building has Cape Dutch features although it has been altered over the years. The Farmhouse style is supported by the magnificent country setting in which the house is found.

OPPOSITE *Paddocks and green pastures with horses and cows are typical of the Farmhouse-style exterior.*

FARMHOUSE

A Farmhouse garden, as its name suggests, belongs to and develops naturally in the countryside – but it is also a style seen in some fairly densely populated urban environments. In essence, it is a down-to-earth approach that features beautifully tended vegetable and herb gardens, orchards, duck ponds and aviaries; the larger spreads may also incorporate meadows, paddocks and stables, perhaps chicken coops and even cow sheds.

Obviously the property has to be extensive enough to accommodate these space-consuming elements, and it helps if there is a natural supply of water nearby. Many homeowners who have espoused the style enjoy riparian rights, enabling them to draw water from an adjacent river or stream. Alternatively, you may decide to sink a borehole or, if the water table is high enough, to dig a well.

If you want to keep animals (horses, perhaps even donkeys, pigs or cows), you may need a permit from the relevant local authority, and the numbers you are allowed may be restricted.

While there is an emphasis on growing things for their practical value, the average contemporary Farmhouse gardener is not restricted by the financial constraints suffered by the early cottagers. There is enough space here, and by implication enough money and independence, to make gardening a pleasant occupation. Fruit and vegetables are grown in separate areas, away from the colourful flowerbeds that add charm to the front of the house – though this does not mean that these functional plots have to be relegated to a secluded corner. On the contrary, they are an important ingredient of the total scheme.

There is room on the property for the inclusion of smaller garden areas designed in other specific styles (for instance, a Victorian rose garden), but the typical Farmhouse garden's real distinction is its rolling lawns and informal flower beds. While the entrance may be defined by pillars and a low wall, post-and-rail fences are more common here, and around other areas (paddocks and so on). Patios and terraces are designed for a relaxed lifestyle.

Layout

Design and composition will be determined largely by the size of the property, by the activities it accommodates and by the style of the house itself. And if the property is indeed a farm, existing outbuildings will have to be taken into account, as well as the location of patios and verandahs used for entertainment.

Generally, though, animals will be housed away from the main dwelling, with the paddock area sited frequently next to stables or cow sheds.

Flowerbeds line the driveway and surround the house, bringing welcome colour and fragrance to the scene. If there is space, a special cut-flower garden (arranged in rows rather like vegetables) may also be included. A generous vegetable garden, also planted in orthodox rows, is located out of sight, while the herb garden (which, although often informal, may be of any style; see page 179) is best established close to the kitchen for convenience. Fruit trees can be confined to a separate orchard, though often they are also integral to the general garden plan. Fruit-bearing climbers – grape vines, Chinese gooseberries, granadillas and so on – are planted over pergolas and informal climbing frames; strawberries are often grown in pots.

Patios and verandahs lead directly to hardy green lawns which, for practical reasons, are sometimes terraced. Rockeries are a common feature on sloping ground. A swimming pool is usually located fairly close to the house.

Colour and plants

While interior Farmhouse-style colours are fresh but faded, those outside are bright and busy. Any combination of hues may be chosen, although a harmonious mix is preferable. Fragrant plants and potted herbs scent the air and there is a tranquil, friendly feel about the place.

Generally speaking, it is the more hardy exotics and the indigenous species – those that will survive adverse weather conditions, including drought, and which generally require little maintenance – that form the basis of this kind of garden.

Agapanthus, of which there are several types, is commonly planted along lengthy driveways; the

RIGHT *Paddocks and stables are sited beyond the landscaped garden of a suburban Farmhouse-style home.*

OPPOSITE
ABOVE *A gregarious gaggle of geese are at home on the hardy green lawn of a modern home.*

BELOW *Established rose bushes, as well as a row of standard roses and beds of yellow and white bearded irises, form an attractive backdrop to one of the duck ponds at Freshwoods, a farm in Elgin in South Africa's Cape Province.*

scrambling shrub plumbago is often used as an informal hedge; various daisies, gazanias and pelargoniums (both scented and flowering) are incorporated into beddings.

Plants that attract birds and bees (see page 175) are also included in the scheme.

In the authentic farmstead garden, large beds may be set aside for colourful annuals – but this is a high-maintenance operation, and much will depend on whether you have the time, or labour, to cope.

Surfaces and materials

Natural materials, preferably those found in the area, are often featured in the Farmhouse garden. Pine rings, for instance, may be used for a casual patio or outdoor steps; rocks and uncut stone for low retaining walls and barbecues.

Wood is a good surface finish (both inside and outside the farmstead), commonly used for such simple structures as pergolas. However, timber decking is not generally appropriate unless incorporated around a pool built on a slope.

Patios are brick paved, although *in situ* concrete, coloured with a suitable paint, is acceptable if the area is covered. Hardwearing railway sleepers are often used for steps.

Seating and structures

Built-in units are not usual in the Farmhouse-style garden, though timber may be used for seating around a large, mature tree. Free-standing is the order of the day: old teak and oak benches, cane chairs and, if there is a generously proportioned and covered verandah, even old upholstered armchairs. In the garden itself, wooden park-type benches and precast concrete or cast-iron designs are left to weather naturally.

Domestic animals and poultry will need outbuildings of one kind or another (see page 173), but for the rest there are not many structures in the typical Farmhouse garden. Pergolas may feature over patios or walkways, and a children's playground, complete with swings, sandpit and a climbing frame, may also be incorporated.

Where there are terraces, you will need steps and balustrades. These are generously proportioned and often painted white.

Features and finishing touches

Ornamentation is not a priority in this type of garden, although a fountain, bird-bath or a simple sundial are appropriate if located close to the main house or outdoor living area.

Containers may be grouped on the patio or terrace, adding a splash of colour.

PART · TWO

DESIGN FOR OUTDOOR LIVING

Designing the outdoor area poses a creative challenge,
but one that is compounded by many practical considerations.
The basic design will involve a general planting plan, the
preparation of various ground surfaces, the provision of shelter,
and the installation of lighting for both safety and night-time
attractiveness. Colour and texture, as well as more ornamental
decoration, will also feature prominently.

Once you have decided on the basic character of your garden,
the planting programme will have to be drawn up in detail.
Among the factors to be borne in mind at this stage are the
various functions you want the outdoor area to fulfil, and the
types of fencing, walling and paving you envisage.

*The outdoor area of this unusual Mediterranean-style home,
perched on a steep hill, has been carefully planned to make full use
of all available garden space.*

A *beautifully manicured garden with a predominantly pink colour scheme and informal approach to beds.*

OPPOSITE
ABOVE LEFT   *A steeply sloping property has been terraced to incorporate a gum pole stairway and stepping stone paths.*

ABOVE RIGHT   *A stepping stone pathway leads through an informal bed, providing access between two lawned areas of a tropical garden.*

BELOW LEFT   *Here, careful attention has been paid to the eventual size of trees and shrubs placed towards the back of this informal bed.*

BELOW RIGHT   *A combination of surfaces and plants creates a well-planned tapestry of pattern, texture and form.*

PLANNING AND PLANTING

Designing a garden demands a lot of patience, since you will have to wait for most of the larger plants to establish themselves before its character can begin to take shape. While you can indeed achieve instant colour and effect – by planting a combination of reasonably sized shrubs, perennials and annuals – it is nevertheless essential, at the outset, to decide on a specific layout and design. Moreover, you will also need to visualize changes brought about as the garden develops.

Gardens constantly alter as they grow, and unless you have a clearly defined plan of action from the very beginning, and carry it out in an ordered manner, you will find it very difficult to create a coherent, aesthetically pleasing scheme. Instead, you are likely to finish up with a hotch-potch of plants and an obviously unco-ordinated garden design.

Take account of the *eventual* size of shrubs and trees: unless you calculate their needs at maturity they will crowd the space you have allowed. Consider colour and texture to create a co-ordinated mix of foliage and flowers. Establish a clear idea of where paths, walls, recreation and service areas, swimming pool and so on are to go: indecision at the beginning will cost money, time and effort.

This does not mean that the entire property has to be landscaped in one all-out operation. Indeed, unless yours is a tiny garden, or unless you have an unusually generous budget, it would be preferable to tackle one section at a time. But you do need to have the overall design in mind from the start.

In short, careful thought and logical planning will enable you to develop a well-knit tapestry of colour, texture, form and function.

The plan
The basic principles of garden planning are universal; the emphases will, however depend on your particular needs and preferences.

Do you want a low-maintenance property? Or one in which the focus is on outdoor living? Would you like a wealth of cut flowers for the interior of your home? If you have young children, you will need somewhere for them to run and play. If they have tricycles and scooters, consider an area with a hard surface. If you entertain a lot, give thought to a patio, a barbecue area, or perhaps a gazebo beside the swimming pool. Other parts of the property may be allocated to vegetables, to a herb garden, perhaps – if space allows – to a small orchard.

Most gardens are of course designed with more than one purpose in mind, and there are usually separate areas delineated for the various activities. Decide at the outset where screen walls and hedges are to be located; where you want the washing line; and where any structures (barbecues or pergolas, arbours, carports and so on) are to be built, either now or in the future. All these factors will affect the overall planting plan.

Layout

The shape and size of the property will, obviously, have a direct bearing on your garden scheme. But whatever the proportions, when it comes to laying out – and this is relevant whether you are planning from scratch or altering an established area – it is important to consider all the practical and aesthetic aspects at the outset, just as you would if you were planning the interior of your home.

However, rather than consider each area in detail and in isolation, as you would inside the home (lounge, bedroom, kitchen, bathroom and so on), simply list the plot's various functions (as we have described in Part Three) and then decide on the best location for each particular space. Look at everything – from the entrance (including exterior gates, doors, and the driveway) to walls, paths and walkways, patios and paving, seating, shelter and outbuildings. Identify sections that will best accommodate a children's play area, a kitchen or herb garden, a swimming pool and, if the property is large enough, perhaps a croquet lawn or tennis court. Do not forget to make provision for essential service areas (for rubbish bins, washing lines, wood or coal storage), a compost heap and so forth.

LEFT *A well-planned service area leading from the driveway has been imaginatively planted to add colour and charm to what could have been a dull, dreary area.*

OPPOSITE *A riot of colour has been achieved by planting a mix of shrubs, perennials and a mass of annuals in generous, informal beds.*

Ideally, work on a site plan drawn to at least a 100:1 scale on graph paper. Sketch in the house and all other existing features: rocks, trees, bushes and shrubs, mounds, hollows (even if these are to be filled in); indicate the direction of the prevailing wind; identify view sites so that you can use them to best advantage, planting to draw attention to the aspect rather than detract from or compete with it. If beds have already been established, make sure you mark these on the plan, making a note of both the plants you wish to keep and those you intend removing or transplanting.

Before you finalize the layout, analyze the wind patterns, and ensure you know which areas of the garden are shady and which get full sun.

Design

Once you have decided on the basic layout, consider the design, as a whole, in more detail. Do you intend following a particular theme or to plant in a specific style? If there are variations in level, will retaining walls be required, and will you need to build steps to get from one point to another? Is the slope such that terraces, with stepped beds between them, would be more effective? What materials will you use for pathways, patios, terraces and other parts of the garden floor?

The design of any landscape will of course depend, to a large degree, on local conditions: the weather and seasonal changes, the type of soil (see Plant Choice, further on), the shape and size of the plot, and the gradients of the site. If yours is a sloping property, you may wish to level certain areas, but it is often preferable to use embankments creatively rather than flatten the ground to form a dull plateau with no undulations.

A popular design concept is the 'garden within a garden'. This idea is generally better suited to a large area, but even a modest-sized, narrow plot can incorporate it with, for example, small sections linked together through archways or along pathways that wind behind hedges or established bushes. An area close to the kitchen may be devoted to herbs and a few vegetables; a section adjacent to the front door perhaps to roses or other fragrant plants, and, if you have children, a portion within their play area to a miniature garden filled with pretty flowers and quick-growing vegetables (see pages 65-66).

By creating interesting nooks and crannies and 'rooms' within the garden, you will introduce an appealing element of surprise and, at the same time, make the property appear larger than it really is.

Some property owners are lucky enough to have unobstructed view sites; the rest of us must simply make the best of what we have. If you are surrounded by houses and want to remove them from line of sight, the usual procedure is to plant around the boundary. If you can, though, make sure you retain at least a glimpse of neighbouring trees and established shrubs. This will extend perspective and, again, visually enlarge your garden.

If there is a point where mountain, sea or some other attraction is visible, a deliberate break in the planting arrangement will enhance the scheme: even though you may not want to to create an Eastern-style garden, the Japanese design philosophy – that part of it which allows you to look into the distance and so escape the restrictiveness of a small space – can still be adapted with great effect (see page 25) in many garden schemes.

Hard landscaping

Once you are reasonably sure of the overall design, landscaping can begin. This involves preparing the site for planting (termed 'soft landscaping'), as well as the erection of fences, construction of walls, the laying of paving, the preparation of paths and so on. If you are planning to incorporate a pool, it should, ideally, be installed prior to planting (though this is not always financially feasible, and it may have to be included in a longer plan of action).

Hard landscaping itself involves all the 'hard' materials: bricks, rocks and stone, timber, slate, concrete and so on, which will be used for structural and other work. While these materials tend to be expensive, it is hard landscaping which provides the foundation of your garden, a basic structure, or shell, ready for planting.

BELOW *Trees have been used to create a natural barrier between paddocks and homestead garden on a cattle farm.*

BOTTOM *A charming property, originally designed by the renowned British architect, Sir Herbert Baker, who utilized the popular Victorian concept of a 'garden within a garden'.*

The choice of materials will depend largely on personal preference and budget. However, it is always advisable to ensure some kind of visual link between garden and house in order to create harmony of colour and maintain a certain consistency of materials. If yours is a facebrick house, garden walls should be built from the same type of facebrick; if the house is plastered, paint boundary and screen walls the same colour. If you want more variety, choose a hue that complements or contrasts the house colour (see page 77) and is in keeping with the general colour theme of the garden.

An architectural link is just as important. An internal arch, visible through the front door, may be mirrored by an arch outside the door, or a sequence of pillars may be continued from the inside to the outside. If there are decorative embellishments on the exterior of the house, try to repeat these within the garden – on walls, pillars or perhaps archways.

While the messy structural work progresses, take the opportunity to prepare the soil for planting, and lay out your beds and borders according to the design you have chosen.

Plant choice

All plants have their own shape, form and purpose. They may be organized to enclose, shelter, screen or to provide a colourful backdrop for outdoor living. If they are used within a carefully contrived framework, you will create an environment that will both meet your practical needs and provide you with endless pleasure.

Many amateur gardeners choose plants for quite the wrong reasons: they simply like them and insist on having them in spite of inappropriate soil or climatic conditions, or perhaps the plants are cheap, or even free (perhaps rescued from a friend who has no further use for them). Moreover, homeowners without gardening experience tend to think of flowers only in terms of providing colour in general rather than of their place in the a more ordered and well planned colour scheme (see pages 75-83).

When deciding what to plant, visualize the eventual shape and size of trees, shrubs and flowers. The relevant information is usually given on plants

stocked by nurseries, and will certainly be found in good gardening books (see page 205). A very broad rule of thumb is to allow a distance between plants equal to their mature height.

Just as you would draw elevations when designing a house, so sketch the patterns you would like plants to create in the various areas of the garden. Plants towards the back of a bed will usually be taller than those at the inner edge. Similarly, a grouping around a tree will decrease in height as the plants spread out over the bed.

A *variety of* proteaceae *feature in this predominantly indigenous South African garden created by an amateur gardener from America.*

Once you are happy with the general impression, consider colour and texture (see page 83), and only then decide which particular species will both meet your needs and best adapt to the conditions and macro-climate in your garden.

The effect you wish to create will determine whether you group several of the same species and colour together, or whether you mix plants each of a different shape, height and breadth (see Types and Themes, pages 63-73).

Finally, the choice of species you opt for will depend on locality as well as the nature of the soil and the wind. If one corner of the garden is particularly windy, concentrate on plants that are hardy and low growing or choose shrubs that are indigenous to your area. Similarly, a bed that is in full sun, a shade garden and so forth, will each demand appropriate types of plantings.

When planning from scratch, it may be necessary to maintain temporary beds until the garden begins to mature. These may perhaps be in a space which will eventually be shaded by a large tree but is now just a sapling (the area can be planted with shade-loving shrubs at a much later stage). Or you may decide to plant grass – a relatively cheap and quick-growing ground cover – in a place that will eventually be paved, or which you have earmarked as the site of the future swimming pool.

If you have areas of bare ground and cannot afford to do much with them, an inventive solution is to plant out a mass of annuals which thrive in your area – perhaps daisies, allysum or candytuft, poppies and cornflowers – to create a carpet of colour. Special meadow seed is also available – invaluable if you want to create this kind of wild garden (see pages 72-73).

BELOW LEFT *Pink and white allysum effectively cover bare ground around standard roses and a covered swimming pool pump and filter.*

BELOW *Daisies create an inexpensive floral carpet of colour in an undeveloped corner of a garden.*

Order of planting

Many homeowners prefer to tackle individual sections of the garden one at a time. This is a logical approach, though bear in mind that one should plant most, if not all of the trees – which are permanent and take a long time to establish themselves – at an early stage. The same principle applies to hedges and boundary shrubs, which also take longer to grow, and which will only provide privacy once they are on their way to maturity. In short, trees and shrubs are the skeleton of the garden, and you should aim to plant as many of them as you can during the earliest stages.

For owners of new homes, a lawn is invariably high on the priority list. Turf is practical and will instantly conceal a dusty, dirty and unsightly yard, but do not be tempted to cover *all* the exposed ground in an attempt to neaten the outdoor area in the shortest possible space of time.

Annuals are also an 'instant' solution, but bear in mind that they are transient and will have to be removed once they have finished flowering – usually after two to six months. A good way to create immediate colour (and to fill gaps) is to put down annuals between newly planted shrubs and perennials. The annuals will die off long before the other plants mature (and can, of course, be easily replaced the following year if necessary).

If you intend planting in sections, tackle the area around the front door or entrance first – this, after all, is where initial impressions are created. If a kitchen garden is a priority (see pages 177-183), lay this out next. Vegetables and herbs do not take long to grow and you will soon reap rich rewards. The surrounds of patios, pools and other outdoor entertainment areas will probably come next – but, again, it all depends on your particular priorities.

Juniper bushes, roses and trees create the framework of this charming informal garden.

A *white colour theme dominates a formal rose garden.*

OPPOSITE
ABOVE LEFT   *Although the lines of these flowerbeds are curved, the garden design is symmetrical.*

ABOVE RIGHT   *An unusual water garden designed by Patrick Watson flows across the driveway into a pond.*

BELOW LEFT   *A pretty little flower garden with a neatly clipped lawn and lots of beds.*

BELOW RIGHT   *Two bronze statues stand guard at the entrance to an English Country-style garden with herbaceous borders. Design: Ian Ford.*

TYPES AND THEMES

Designers of all kinds find it helpful to have some sort of a *theme* to follow, and in the garden the thematic possibilities are limitless.

A particular style may be your theme (see Part One), inspired perhaps by the architecture of the house. Or you may prefer an indigenous garden, a wild garden or perhaps a flower garden.

Alternatively, you might like the idea of using colour as a theme (see page 82).

For variety, your garden may (if, of course, it is large enough) be divided into areas each with its own theme – a rose garden, a herb garden perhaps, a rock garden, a water garden, a sunken or secret garden and so forth, all on the same property.

One has an enormous choice when it comes to theme. By contrast, however, there are only two basic garden *types*: formal and informal.

Type

If you decide to follow a particular style, this will, to a large extent, determine whether your garden is formal or informal. For instance, a Cape Dutch or European-style garden will be formal, while one that is planted in the less rigid Farmhouse or Cottage style will be quite the opposite.

It is primarily the layout that will determine type, but of course the various structures and other individual features will need to be in keeping. Steps in a formal garden, for example, will follow straight lines and may incorporate pillars and balustrades on either side. They will usually be built from brick, concrete or planed timber. By contrast, informal steps will be constructed randomly from stone or perhaps railway sleepers and will have a more rustic appeal. Or their casual informality may be conferred by their shape – perhaps gently curved to complement the shapes of flowerbeds and pathways.

The design of water features and finishing touches (statuary, pots, benches and so on) should also complement the garden type selected.

Formal The formal garden is characterized by straight lines, symmetry, and a carefully planned balance. Clipped hedges and topiary (see page 116) fit in well. If lawned areas are incorporated, they must be kept well mown. Ornamentation and finishing touches (see pages 115-116) should be bold and preferably classical in form. Sundials, statues, pots and the like must all be in keeping with the grandness and formality of the look.

Traditionally palaces, chateaux and castles all had vast formal gardens to match their splendour, and many of the world's most celebrated estates – those of Versailles and Hampton Court, for instance – are of this type. They featured grand parterres (see page 204) or intricate knot gardens on terraces. Some of the greatest French gardens (or potagers, see page 204, like that found at Villandry in the Loire Valley) of the 15th and 16th centuries featured fruit and vegetables laid out in elaborate formal patterns similar to the grand parterre, each bed bordered by a low, well-clipped hedge.

The Victorian version involved a series of rigidly shaped carpet beds packed with plants arranged to form an attractive mosaic pattern. The Victorians also favoured the formal rose garden. The fragrant plants were laid out geometrically, with perhaps four paths leading from the centre to each corner or along the sides of a formal path or 'walk'. Decorative arches and classic support structures were also incorporated into the garden design.

Herb gardens, too, were (and often still are) planted in a formal fashion (see page 179).

Informal Gentle curves and irregular flowerbeds typify the informal garden. Avoid straight lines and allow plants to spill over onto lawns and paving to add to the casual, flexible look.

The informal garden layout commonly incorporates island beds, often planned around existing features such as trees and established shrubs, and taking the natural rise and fall of the ground into account. They may be of any size and shape, but there should be plenty of space between them or the effect will be contrived. Wild gardens, woodlands and meadows are, of course, also informal.

Historically, the two 19th-century garden-makers most closely associated with this specific type are Gertrude Jekyll and William Robinson (see pages 203 and 204). It was they who urged a move away from the formal designs and rigid planting so popular up to then. Their choice of plant also tended to look less contrived and more natural, and of course their gardens were much easier to maintain although frequent weeding was necessary.

OPPOSITE *The beautifully laid out formal parterre at the 17th century Tuynhuys in Cape Town was restored by the South African Government more than 20 years ago according to a design prepared by G.T. Fagan Architects.*

ABOVE LEFT *An adventure hut set on stilts above a tropical garden provides a perfect place for children to play.*

ABOVE RIGHT *A simple gum pole frame supports a wooden swing and knotted rope.*

Theme

As mentioned, there are many possible garden themes, the most common being those based on style (see Part One). The indigenous garden and the wilderness are also popular, although wild gardens are more often located in only one section of a property, usually some distance from the house and entertainment areas.

For centuries gardens have been divided into various portions, each of which has a different use – or theme. Thus herbs may be the theme of one area, roses of another, and water of a third.

A *children's garden* Young children need constant supervision but, as they get older, they become more and more adventurous and independent and need to be stimulated.

In a moderate climate, there are many ways of creating exciting outdoor play areas (see pages 197-199); climbing frames, rope ladders, swings, slides and sandpits are just some of the possibilities. In addition, the garden can help children to appreciate the wondrous miracles of nature.

The task of preparing a children's garden is often simplified if you are working within the confines of an established property. This will depend, though, on whether it was well planned and properly planted. If so, there will be secluded corners; and shrubs and bushes that are so well established that they provide almost jungle-like conditions; and large, mature trees that are perfect for tree houses (which may simply be a sturdy, wooden platform nailed into the branches or something as sophisticated as a Wendy house in the air).

On the other hand, you will also need some open, grass-covered space for the children to play and run on, and perhaps a few sunlit beds in which they can plant their own, quick-growing vegetables and pretty flowers for cutting.

Even if there is not enough room for expansive lawns, most gardens have the space to accommodate some play equipment. Enclose this area with a screen or hedge of some kind (see pages 86-87) and designate a portion – at very least a narrow bed around the perimeter – for planting.

Just as sections within an entire property are set aside for various activities and functions, so too are those within the ideal children's garden. Try and incorporate a miniature flower garden; a small vegetable garden; the play area; perhaps a pet's corner with a rabbit-hutch or aviary.

Colour An immensely wide range of attractive effects can be created by using colour as a garden theme. For instance, you could opt for a limited combination of colours – pink and white or yellow and blue, for example – or try varying tones of just one hue rather than a random mix. Although it is not essential to strive for a particular style, English Country, Victorian and Cottage gardens all rely to some extent on the use of a colour theme.

Whatever the choice, though, it is important to have a basic understanding of colour harmony and contrast if the scheme is to be really successful (see pages 75-83).

Bright bands of colour have been created by planting groups of annuals, including marigolds and petunias.

The single-colour theme border was popularized by the eminent British garden designer and author Gertrude Jekyll (see page 82 and page 203), who worked on more than 300 gardens between 1880 and 1932. It was largely her training in painting and embroidery that gave her a special appreciation of the qualities of form, texture and the colour of plants, and enabled her to create beautiful combinations in the garden. And much can be learnt from her plans, most which survive – on paper, at least.

Amateur gardener Vita Sackville-West (see page 204), is legendary for her entirely White Garden at her home, Sissinghurst, in the English county of Kent. One of the best-known English gardens of the 20th century, it features a series of linked but independent areas, perpetuating the idea of a variety of 'rooms' within the garden.

You could in fact take the concept further by creating a series of mini-gardens each with its own colour theme. To achieve this, paths lead you from one to the other, each of which will have its own, dramatically distinctive impact.

However, creating a garden – or indeed simply a border – with a colour theme needs careful thought and planning. It is not enough merely to choose plants that will flower within the chosen colour range. Consider flowering months (not everything will bloom at one time) and foliage, remembering that when there are no flowers on the plants, it will often be the varied texture and colour of leaves that will create the interest.

A charming white garden features a typical Victorian-style gazebo at the end of a brick path.

Flowers An all-time favourite, the flower garden is incorporated in many garden styles, especially English Country and Cottage. To succeed, it is important to take into account all the characteristics of the flowering plants you choose – height, colour, flowering time, lifespan and so on – in order to achieve a continuous, long-lasting show. The most effective approach is to combine perennials with a few shrubs, bulbs and annuals. Plant in autumn for spring flowers; and in late spring for summer blooms, many of which will last until late autumn.

Ensure, too, that shapes contrast with one another for variety, and mix species with different leaf textures. Remember that many colourful flowers and shrubs are also sweet-smelling and that fragrance, like colour, attracts pollinating bees and butterflies and will generally add to the attractiveness of the garden as a whole.

While commercial flower gardeners usually plant in rectangular beds, just as market gardeners do, you may well prefer a more informal approach.

Raised flowerbeds are a practical option as they enable you to apply extra compost, peat and so on. If the beds are 400-600 mm (16-24 in), it will also be easier to see the display of all the plants. A traditional raised bed will have a permanent border defining its edges.

The vicarage garden (which developed during the 19th century) was devised to provide a constant supply of flowers for the church. To re-create this kind of arrangement you will, for practical reasons, need to divide the garden into square and rectangular beds, the whole forming a regular framework which may be viewed, and be accessible from, all sides. Each bed is edged with a low hedge – cotton lavender (*Santolina*) or box (*Buxus*), for instance – and planted with one type (or group) of plants rather than with a mixture. Paths around the beds may be brick, concrete, laterite, pebbled or even grassed (although this last is not usual).

One of the most famous flower gardens of all time was created by the Impressionist painter Claude Monet, at his Giverny home in France. Here flowers were planted in broad, sweeping groups of colour with spectacular success.

An indigenous garden This will appeal to anyone who loves the untamed look of a wild garden (see further on). Not only is it a reasonably low-maintenance and easy-to-care-for arrangement but, like all other kinds of 'wild' garden, it will also tend to attract birds, bees and butterflies to create both interest and pleasure.

The main focus is on roses in this delightful pink, red, white and green flower garden.

An indigenous garden, though, needs time to become established: planting proceeds gradually, in an informal way, so that the mature garden appears to have developed naturally. However, an outdoor area created in this fashion will ultimately be less demanding – indigenous plants are more likely to survive adverse weather conditions, including drought, and thus generally need less maintenance.

While some gardeners may choose to plant species that are endemic to their own area, there is nothing to prevent you cultivating plants from other regions. It seems to be common belief that many indigenous plants are territorial, but this is not necessarily so. For instance a number of tropical species, including the wild banana (*Ensete ventricosum*) and various strelizias, flourish in sub-tropical areas.

Although purists will tend to banish exotic cultivars altogether in favour of native species, you may prefer to have the best of both worlds, creating a separate indigenous section within the garden as a whole. This may simply be an area of indigenous flora or an embankment planted in naturally rocky areas (see Rocks, below).

Rocks Useful on sloping plots, rock gardens and rockeries are relatively easy to maintain. They are planted with bushes, small shrubs and, generally, with hardy species that are not suitable in other parts of the garden.

However, the creation of a successful rock – and indeed, of any – garden takes time and thought.

An effective garden of this type should not look contrived but will rather resemble a natural outcrop of rock and, for this reason, the size and type of stone chosen is important. Weathered rocks found in the area are the most suitable.

BELOW LEFT *Indigenous plants predominate in this charming garden, which nestles beneath the Constantiaberg near the world-famous Kirstenbosch Gardens in Cape Town, South Africa.*

BELOW *Natural rock plays a vital role in this man-made wetland. Design: Patrick Watson.*

It is not enough to simply scatter a jumble of stone randomly over the area chosen; and rocks must *never* be placed on mounds of soil. Rather, to create the authentic look, they should give the impression of rising from a solid base. Avoid too many variations in height, and fill the gaps between the rocks with soil so that they are partially submerged and thus appear to have occurred naturally. About two-fifths of the garden should be rock, and, if you are creating it on flat ground, do not raise its height by more than about 50 cm (20 in).

A rather outmoded variation of the rock garden is the alpine garden, which imitates a mountain environment. Such a garden will be sited on sloping ground; choice of plants will depend on the region in which you live, and should as a rule be indigenous to the area. In the south-western Cape of South Africa, for instance, a rock or alpine garden looks best planted with proteas (most of which are shrubs), ericas (of which there are many species), local grasses, pelargoniums, everlastings, mesembryanthemums (vygies) and lilies, including agapanthus, aloes, red-hot pokers (*Kniphofia praecox*) and so on.

An advantage of an artificially created rock garden is that you can mix species that grow in different types of soil. This is effected by using the rocks almost as planters.

It is seldom appropriate to allot all the space on a property to a rock garden or rockery. Choose an area which is well drained and exposed to the sun and, ideally, away from trees and other large shrubs.

A *rose garden* While roses are an all-time favourite, there are very few homeowners today who are willing to devote the entire garden to this family. Nevertheless, while it is quite acceptable to include roses in mixed beds and rockeries, the trend is to separate them from most other plants – though perhaps mixing in a ground cover (pennyroyal – *Mentha pulegium* – or lacy alyssum, for instance).

BELOW LEFT *Broad brick steps lead to a large formal rose garden packed with a variety of species and colours.*

BELOW *A beautifully engineered artificial water feature created along a natural rock course. Plants are largely indigenous to the area.*

OPPOSITE
ABOVE *A stepping stone path curves past an informal bed planted with roses.*

BELOW *A formal rose garden forms part of an outdoor design created in imitation of the English Country genre.*

This separation has the backing of the experts, who maintain that roses – considered the aristocrats of the garden – are best grown, and seen, on their own. However, there are also practical considerations: apart from anything else, it is more convenient for pruning and feeding to have them all in one place. The visual effect in spring and summer is also more dramatic.

The size of the rose garden is not important. Rose lovers who have the space are able to plant these much revered shrubs and climbers over a wide area of garden; and those with small gardens in just a little patch where their fragrance and beauty may be enjoyed. Residents of compact townhouses, or even of apartments with balconies, can usually grow them successfully in containers.

The conditions of the site are, however, significant. Roses grow best where they will get full sun for most of the day, but where they will not be battered by the wind. Although they are said to like clay, the soil must be well-drained. A medium loam is best.

The type of rose garden you decide to plant will depend, as always, on the style of the house and on the layout of the rest of the garden.

If you have settled on a Victorian-style garden, a formal rose walk will be in perfect keeping. Standard roses may be planted down either side, with shrubs filling the beds. If the walk leads to the boundary of the property, place a period sundial or statue at the end and plant climbing roses behind to create an attractively appropriate backdrop.

A formal rose garden is another possibility, providing of course you have the space. A typical plan will comprise four or five lines of roses planted in an oval shape (increasing in height to the outside), with eight standards spaced evenly around the perimeter. A path around this 'crown' leads off from the four cardinal points.

Often, too, gardens designed in the Victorian manner feature a classical support of one sort or another – an arch or other framework, usually made of metal. Alternatively, rambling roses or climbers may be trained along swags of rope supported by sturdy posts, creating interesting outlines at the back or around the perimeter of a formal bed.

If yours is a modern house, or the rest of the garden has been laid out in an informal way, neither a traditional nor a formal rose garden or walk will be appropriate. Instead, the answer is to plant in simple beds for maximum effect.

Your selection of rose types will be dictated by the effects you wish to create. Some species will give more fragrance than others; some are more suitable for the vase and, of course, colour will also be a major factor to consider.

A *wild garden* Such a garden appeals to the romantic in us, conjuring images of red poppies and blue cornflowers swaying in the wind, or wild grass heads shimmering against a hazy summer sky. Or perhaps it evokes the warm, sunny days and lazy lifestyle of more carefree times. Whatever the reason for the attraction, these low-maintenance gardens have enjoyed world-wide popularity in recent years – though in fact there is nothing new about the wild garden. According to historians, a medieval lawn was more like a meadow than the smooth, green ground cover we are more familiar with, a fragrant carpet of herbs and flowers similar to those created in contemporary wild-flower meadows. And in 17th-century England, wilderness or heath gardens of varying types were commonplace.

They also had their place in the 19th century. In his best-selling book, *The Wild Garden* (published in 1870), plantsman William Robinson (see Informal, above, and page 204) described the wild garden as one where plants from other countries could be successfully planted and left to grow without further cost or care. He wrote that 'a pretty plant in a free state is more attractive than any garden denizen'. Incidentally, though, the flowers themselves were not necessarily 'wild' varieties: rather, they were grown in an informal fashion in a garden meadow or woodland tucked away in a secluded area. In fact many of the plants grown in Victorian 'wild' gardens were exotics which had to be carefully tended!

The basic character, and the success, of any 'meadow' is dependent on the grass species that is either present or has been planted. Preferably, encourage wild and ornamental grasses.

One of the common problems in creating a wild meadow – unless you are starting with virgin ground – is that strongly growing lawn grasses tend to swamp the flowers. The idea of planting bulbs in a grassed area is an appealing one, but the effect will be ruined if the grass needs frequent mowing.

On the market are special meadow-mix seeds that contain wild grasses as well as flowers that bloom at different times of the year. As each batch dies back – seeding itself – the next comes through. Other seed blends are also available, including a poppy mix, which will give a dramatically bright, seasonal show of colour. Alternatively, mix your own, combining a suitable range of primarily wild flowers.

In theory, meadows are easy to maintain, although some weeding and mowing is usually necessary. Some garden experts also advocate top dressing in late spring and severe mowing in autumn to neaten the area and give the spring flowers a good chance to develop. But if yours is a sizeable meadow, it may be advantageous to mow paths through the area to create walkways.

Of course, as we have noted, a bonus is that the wild garden will tend to attract birds, insects and butterflies. Similarly, a 'wetland' (a natural water garden), will also be a magnet for birds, as well as for frogs and other wildlife. Fish will help reduce numbers of unwanted insects.

OPPOSITE A *beautifully contrived wild garden appears to have evolved quite naturally.*

BELOW A *natural woodland given form with constructed paths and steps and some additional planting.*

Red poppies will add a splash of colour to any garden.

OPPOSITE
ABOVE LEFT *A variety of annuals create a riot of colour alongside a brick paved walkway.*

ABOVE RIGHT *Impatiens, available in a wide range of reds, oranges, pinks and white, will usually thrive in lightly shaded conditions.*

BELOW LEFT *Pink and purple is an effective and popular colour theme for borders.*

BELOW RIGHT *A small, informal bed planted with pink and yellow flowers makes a charming feature beside a shimmering blue swimming pool.*

COLOUR

Just as colour is integral to interior design, so this magical tool may be used outside the house with a multitude of effects. Where the two differ, though, is that the exterior colour arrangement is forever changing. Plants grow and each season confers its distinctive hues; the quality and nature of light differ almost from hour to hour: within a span of a single day the sky may turn from deep dusky orange to many shades of blue and grey.

Nature has provided us with an unbelievable palette of colours. You will, however, have to make some choices, as too many hues will tend to lack harmony. This does not mean that you cannot mix colours: indeed some of the most beautiful gardens contain a wide variety of hues. But it does mean avoiding a jumble of colour and those combinations that will appear disorganised, those that jar and those that are plainly uninspiring.

The colour wheel
The colour wheel is a commonly used aid in planning the interior of a home, but few people consider it necessary when laying out a garden. Nevertheless, this basic tool can help you choose combinations that will work well together.

The wheel is simply a spectrum of twelve hues arranged in a circle. It comprises three primary colours (red, yellow and blue), three secondary colours (green, violet and orange, each of which is a combination of two primary colours), and six tertiary colours (each a combination of two of the secondaries).

The natural spectrum is of course continuous, with infinite gradations of each colour. Nevertheless, the colours on the wheel are considered pure hues that, when mixed either with the so-called 'non-colours', black or white or with each other, will produce every other colour, tint and tone.

Generally, colours are classified as being 'warm' or 'cool'. Reds, yellows and orange tend towards the former, blues to the latter. Green, considered Nature's own colour, is essentially fresh, restful, reassuring and soothing, and neither warm nor cool.

The warm colours will tend to advance, indeed to 'leap out' at you, while the cool colours and green will recede. Thus, should you wish to emphasize depth in order to create an illusion of distance (an effective ploy in small spaces), use cool colours in the background with the more vibrant hues in front. The reverse approach applies if you wish to make a vast space appear more intimate.

Analogous An analogous arrangement is one that is harmonious and includes three or four adjacent (and therefore related) colours – red, red-orange, orange and yellow-orange, for example.

In interior design, an analogous scheme generally features a dominant hue. This is not necessarily the case when it comes to the garden, although a small space is often enhanced by the use of one basic colour with two or three related tones.

Moreover, since the range of flowering plants (flowers and shrubs) is so vast – and the selection of colours, therefore, so varied – it is usually preferable to plan for some diversity.

Here, a good option would be to move through the colours of the wheel: a patch of yellows and oranges, for instance, may lead to a bed planted with flowers blooming in shades which vary from orangey-red to violet; nearby, but perhaps separated by a low hedge, violet hues and blues may blend beautifully with green shrubbery. This approach correlates with the teachings of Gertrude Jekyll, one of the greatest British landscape gardeners, who emphasized the importance of colour selection. In designing herbaceous borders – for which she is famous – she showed how colour changes should be introduced in the same gradual manner.

BELOW LEFT *Overgrown flowering pot plants combine beautifully to create a primarily pastel pink patch of colour.*

BELOW *Red verbena and salvia, pink daisies, and mauve and pink impatiens, combine well in a single bed.*

Monochromatic Popular in contemporary interior design, monochromatic colour schemes rely on a single hue which is used with variations of intensity, texture and pattern.

Since green is always present in the garden, no outdoor scheme can be termed strictly monochromatic – unless, of course, it relies on shades of green itself. However, so-called 'single-colour' themes are once again becoming popular (see Colour Themes further on) in garden design.

Complementary A colour scheme that relies on two contrasting hues from opposite sides of the colour wheel is termed complementary. Red, for instance, complements green; yellow complements violet; and blue, orange.

A complementary colour scheme creates an air of vitality, and although too many contrasts can be overpowering, there is little doubt that any garden will be enhanced by a few, especially if one colour is used as an accent.

Characteristics of colour

The qualities of the various colours will enable you to create different moods and feelings within the outdoor area. Some are restful and soothing; others are bright, lively and stimulating. The choice is yours, and dependent on the effect you wish to create.

Red Although it is possibly the most difficult colour to handle on its own, red is dramatic, passionate and, if properly used, can give warmth, boldness and vibrancy to the garden. However, it does not show up well at night.

There are many different shades of red, ranging from burning scarlet to cool maroon (which contains blue) and encompassing a wide variety of plants. Among others, there are deep red roses, scarlet sage (*Salvia splendens*), as well as radiant azaleas, bright red poppies, a variety of anemones, begonias, impatiens, lupins, lobelias, phlox, primulas and velvety petunias; not to forget ever popular geraniums (*Pelargonium* spp.), red poinsettias and richly hued tulips which grow well in humid climates or in a greenhouse.

And it is not just flowers but some varieties of foliage, too, that display these brilliant hues (crotons and coleus, for instance).

There are, of course, many red fruits as well: strawberries, raspberries, cherries, nectarines, plums and grapes. And aubergines, tomatoes, red peppers and chillies also ripen to varying shades of red.

Bold, vibrant red is the most prominent colour in this bed lining a farmhouse driveway.

Pink Related to red, pink is a particularly popular shade for the garden. It is not, however, a hot, fiery colour but rather soft and warm by comparison. There are many variations of pink which, when massed together, produce beautiful effects.

The range of pink flowers is also huge, and includes, among many others, roses, petunias, impatiens, fuchsias, azaleas, geraniums — to name just a few. Blossom, too, is often pink in colour.

Yellow Bright, warm, the universal sunshine colour. Whether or not it is in fashion (and its popularity *does* seem to wax and wane), it seldom fails to produce a feeling of lively cheerfulness.

Yellow flowers, like white, show up well at night, but are especially radiant during the day. The list of planting possibilities is endless: marigolds and daisies, sunflowers (which look glorious in full bloom, but so sad as they wilt away), chrysanthemums, gladioli, cannas, pansies, lilies, petunias, roses and, of course, daffodils for spring.

Yellow is softened by cream and white and, blended, will produce a more sophisticated effect.

Orange Also bright, cheery and warm, orange is an easy colour to introduce into your garden. Not currently popular in interiors, but favoured by gardeners for its vibrancy, often bringing life to dull and dreary outdoor areas.

Since orange is the warmest colour of all, it is often combined with blue to cool the effect. Blue and orange, in fact, is a particularly successful complementary outdoor scheme.

ABOVE *Varying shades of pink combine with a touch of mauve to create a soft, warm effect.*

BELOW *Pale pink hydrangeas complement impatiens of a slightly darker shade.*

There are numerous orange-hued flowers: marigolds, chrysanthemums, snapdragons, pansies, gazanias, various types of lily, certain honeysuckles (which seldom fails to attract sunbirds) and, of course, the magnificent *Strelizia reginae*, which grows particularly well in warmer climates.

Orange is also introduced into the garden during the autumn season, before the leaves begin to fall, and as the leaves change colour (which they will, unless you live in more tropical parts of the world), golds and bronzes will take the place of green.

Brown The colour of Mother Earth, brown signifies fertility – a highly appropriate element in the garden context. And, like green, brown will always be a part of the backdrop that forms your outdoor stage. Stones, rocks, twigs, bark, old stems, soil – all are constantly evident in different shades of this, the ultimate neutral colour.

While brown is present in every outdoor situation, we often add our own touches (especially in the Japanese-style garden; see pages 25-27) by way of terracotta pots, stones and pebbles around container plants or even as features on their own: for example, statues or artworks sculpted out of wood.

Blue Cool and calming, blue is a heavenly garden colour, particularly in summer. In fact, it is interesting that several shades of blue are named after various flowers: for instance there is hyacinth blue, gentian (which, unlike the violet dye, actually has deep blue blooms) and orchid, the pale lavender blue so popular in the 1920s.

ABOVE   *Red hot pokers and roses introduce a cheery atmosphere to the garden.*

BELOW   *A mass of orange flowers add warmth to an interesting water feature.*

Delphiniums, periwinkles, forget-me-nots, lobelias and cornflowers (*Centaurea cyanus*) will all introduce blue to your garden. In addition, several indigenous South African plants boast blue flowers (sometimes with a purple tinge; see below), including agapanthus (in particular *Agapanthus africanus* and *A. campanulatus*), the beautifully transparent beige and blue *gladiolus hyalinus*, glorious sky blue plumbago (P. *auriculata* and P. *capensis*), the autumn flowering *Barleria obtusa* (so often seen on roadsides and embankments), and both kingfisher and blue Marguerite daisies which thrive in warmer climates (*Felicia bergerana* and F. *amelloides*, respectively).

Purple A regal hue, purple is often used successfully as an outdoor colour theme. The choice of tones and tints is huge, ranging from deep purple-reds and purple-pinks to bluish purples that include mauve, lavender, lilac and violet. There is an enormous selection of plants, too, and between them they offer something suitable for every type of garden in every part of the world.

You may prefer to consider irises (specifically *Iris kaempferi*) or agapanthus and purple-flowering ericas (heather); for the herb garden lavender, borage and purple catmint, and for the flower garden foxgloves, phlox, pansies, petunias, violas and Michaelmas daisies (A*ster novi-belgii*).

As both purple and green are receding colours, a purple-planted garden will be sure to project a quiet, restful mood.

Green The colour of nature, green is fresh and soothing. Leaves, grass, moss, a wide range of groundcovers, lichen, river water, even flowers, all come in varying shades of green.

Green flowers are not very common but, if you look around, you will find that they do in fact exist. Hydrangeas (H. *macrophylla*, also called the Christmas flower in the southern hemisphere), for instance, are green-flowering until the tiny florets get their colour in the summer months. Then there is the lime-green version of nicotiana, or tobacco plant and green Bells of Ireland (*Molucella laevis*), and, where available, certain protea species, like P. *scolymocephala*, which has light green-yellow blooms. An attractive lily, *Alstroemeria* P. *psittacina*, bears greenish flowers, although they are also rusty-red in parts with brown spotting inside. Arum lilies occasionally have green spathes.

This combination of greens — dark, light, bright and variegated — create a fresh and soothing look.

Non-colours

Technically, the three non-colours are pure black, white, and grey, which strictly speaking is mixed from black and white. While there are no true non-colours in the garden, their approximation – the forms in which they *are* found – can be very effective, even dramatic, if used well.

White A symbol of purity, white has a distinctive beauty which is hard to surpass, either inside or outside the home. Moreover, it is probably the easiest single colour to handle.

In general, white flowers are considered to be night plants since they show up so well by moonlight, evincing an enchanting magical quality. However, by day white has a pristine freshness that is guaranteed to lighten and lend an elegantly soothing touch to any garden space.

Whenever white is placed between two colours, it will emphasize their true value. If red and violet petunias are mixed in a bed, for instance, the general impression will be one of tertiary red-violet, but plant white petunias between them and their real colours will be revealed.

Alternatively, use white as an accent; or contrive an all-white garden area (see Colour Themes further on), with different heights, shapes and textures introduced for variety.

Black Although not common in the garden, nature's occasional touch of black can add drama and excitement – in a black viola or the black centre of a Black-eyed Susan (*Thunbergia alata*), for instance.

White Iceburg roses complement the cool blue used to paint the exterior of a gracious country home.

Grey The shades of grey found outdoors are generally blue-grey and grey-green rather than the true, colourless, neutral grey that interior designers avoid. The silver birch (*Betula pendula*) or in southern climes, the silver cassia (*Cassia artemisioides*) indigenous to Australia, or the South African silver tree (*Leucadendron argenteum*), all with their subtle accents and highlights, will introduce a little magic to the garden. Certain shrubs; ground cover such as snow-in-summer (*Cerastium tomentosum*); herbs, including *Stachus lanata*, with its ear-shaped, velvety leaves, the various lavenders (both the *Lavandula* and *Santolina* species), and some types of sage, will produce a similarly attractive effect on a smaller scale.

Colour combinations

The way various colours are combined will have a marked impact on the look of your garden. Just as one interior colour will affect another (yellow placed alongside red, for instance, will tend to produce an orangey impression), so too will those displayed outdoors. Moreover, colour tones will change according to the varying position of the sun. Artificial lighting will also have its effect at night.

And it is not just flowers (whether annuals, perennials or flowering shrubs or trees) that combine to create a colour scheme. Indeed leaves, berries, fruit, even bark, all contribute towards the final result, often providing a suitable backdrop. Also important are foliage – of the flowers themselves as well as other plants – and the colours of walls, fences and any garden paving.

If yours is a dark facebrick house, dark green foliage will tend to look dull and lifeless. Rather, if this is the case, choose plants with lighter green or grey leaves that will reflect the light. If on the other hand your house is plastered and painted a pale colour, dark foliage and deep-hued flowers will stand out beautifully.

Colour themes

In practice, few gardens (in contrast to domestic interiors) are organized according to strictly defined colour schemes. Broader colour *themes*, however, are once again popular.

As we have seen, the relationships between colours outdoors are essentially the same as those within the house itself – although green will always be evident. In addition, you will tend to have an earth-toned background.

Tricia Guild, the renowned British designer of gardens, interiors and fabrics, believes the most popular of all colour-theme gardens is the all-white, perhaps best exemplified by that created by amateur gardener Vita Sackville-West and her husband, Sir Harold Nicolson, at Sissinghurst in Kent. Here they combined an infinite variety of whites, with here and there just a touch of pink, blue, cream and silver.

There are, however, numerous other possibilities, including the grouping of large numbers of single-coloured flowers together – an approach thought to have been pioneered by the 18th-century British architect and garden designer Sir William Chambers. Gertrude Jekyll, who popularized the monochromatic border, kept detailed records of her garden plans, including an impressive blue border some 23 m (75 ft) x 3,5 m (12 ft) in extent. She allowed blue flowers to dominate: delphiniums (D. X *belladonna*), gentian sage (*Salvia patens*), phacelia (P. *campanularia*), plumbago (P. *auriculata*). However, white flowering plants – white peas, white lupins, madonna lilies, white hollyhocks and foxgloves – were also included in the border, as were several grasses and foliage – maize, yucca, rue, and a number of hosta species, among them *Hosta sieboldiana*, with its metallic-blue tinged leaves, and H. *plantaginea*, with white, bell-like flowers.

Colour changes

Light, weather conditions, time of day and numerous other factors affect colour. Clear, bright light will show up the true value of any colour, while dim, natural light will tend to neutralize it, and artificial light – night-time illumination – will change it. Moreover, colours do not exist in isolation and different hues will interact, producing harmonious or discordant effects (see Non-colours, above).

The actual shape and texture of a leaf or petal will also influence the quality of colour. For instance, a smooth leaf and a plant with furry leaves will appear to differ, as colour is absorbed more readily by an even surface (see Texture and pattern, below).

Remember, too, that deciduous plants will change colour according to the season, especially in areas that experience cold, frosty winters. The swamp cypress (*Taxodium distichum*), for example, has beautifully fine, brilliantly green, ferny leaves in spring, which turn to a deeper green in summer, to a rich orangey-bronze in autumn, and, finally, when its leaves have fallen, becomes a brown winter skeleton of a tree with an elegant shape.

Texture and pattern

In addition to colour, both texture and pattern have a role to play in the garden. Foliage, particularly, can create texture. Smooth, shiny leaves set against velvety ones, and feathery ferns grown next to stiff, spiky plants, illustrate the interest that can be created by varying textures.

Consider, too, the many different types of flowers: a yellow daisy, marigold or dahlia, a smooth-petalled daffodil or a golden-hued rose. They are slightly different in colour, and it is their particular textures that make them so distinctive.

Pattern, on the other hand, is usually introduced in the process of planting, particularly in the formal garden scheme (see page 63-64).

Size, shape and scale

The juxtaposition of contrasting plants is another very effective device used by many gardeners, including the well-known contemporary British landscaper and author, John Brookes.

Simply by arranging species of different shapes and (eventual) sizes, you will introduce a certain flow and movement to the beds.

But leaf shape and size should also be considered; velvety hosta and gunnera with its huge leaves alongside the thin-leafed agapanthus, for example. Or you may like to opt for a traditional mosaic design – the very ultimate in patterned planting.

ABOVE *An interesting display of colour and texture has been created with a clever combination of shrubs and trees.*

OPPOSITE *White is one of the more popular colour themes, particularly in period gardens.*

An imaginative lattice screen forms a charming backdrop for seating in a Victorian-style garden, and, at the same time, hides a utilitarian shed.

WALLS AND SCREENS

A variety of walls, hedges, screens and fences combine to form the basic framework of the garden. They are used on the boundary of the property for privacy and security, and sometimes to block out unsightly views; to delineate certain areas as independent segments; to provide a protective screen from the elements (wind in particular), and even to reduce noise, which is an important factor if your house is near a major road.

The materials used for walls particularly are as vast and varied as those utilized in the construction of the house itself. Bricks, timber, precast concrete, stone – all have a role to play.

In gardening terms, landscaping is generally categorized as being either 'hard' or 'soft' (see pages 58-59). The erection of walls and fences, paving and anything else which requires solid materials – brick, stone and so on – falls under the former classification, and all planting, including that of hedges, under 'soft landscaping'.

In practice, a well-planned garden will always employ a combination of the two landscaping techniques, combining hard, rigid materials (a stone or brick wall, for instance) with foliage and flowers to provide the vital softening effect.

Fencing

Constructed from either wood or metal and wire, fences are a common and effective means of enclosing a property, even though they are considerably less durable than walls.

There are many types and styles of fencing. A partially solid timber structure will make a good windbreak, although it will not block out noise as effectively as a high wall. A post-and-rail fence will simply define the boundary, while a wire mesh fence will serve the same purpose and offer some security (provided, of course, that it has the height). Well planted, it will also form an effective windbreak.

The type of fence chosen will depend on the style of your outdoor area as well as on function. Post-and-rail is perfect for the Farmhouse garden; a picket fence is more appropriate to the cottagey look, and more delicate bamboo to the Japanese-style exterior. Trellis and lattice-work fences are ideal for the Victorian garden, as is decorative wrought-iron.

If you need solid fencing for the perimeter of your suburban property, consider vertical or woven panels, or palisades (posts nailed to horizontal rails). Another possibility is a wooden stockade of cut timber, railway sleepers or poles.

If you have a swimming pool (see pages 191-192), you may be required by the local authority to fence the area. Here, special galvanized metal fencing is most commonly used, although there is nothing to stop you erecting some other type of fence – provided it is at least 1,2 m high and has no cross-pieces on the outside to tempt a child to climb over. Remember, too, that gates leading into the pool area should also be self-closing and self-locking.

Hedges and plant screens

A screen of foliage is an attractive alternative to brick, stone, concrete, even timber. Rich in pattern and texture, it will filter light and introduce welcome contrast to the garden. Formal hedges and informally planted barriers are both excellent for providing privacy and screening against the wind.

Even though a hedge will take longer to create than a wall, it is the cheaper option, and one which will blend with the environment, providing a good-looking backdrop for other plants. It will also take up less space than most informal borders.

Hedges, a centuries-old means of screening and enclosing, are most common in the formal garden, though they are appropriate to other styles, including the informal Cottage garden.

The type and size of hedge planted will depend on its particular function. A boundary hedge will usually be allowed to grow to a reasonable height, while a hedge around a formal flower bed may be only a few centimetres high. A hedge screening an area within the garden will be about 1,8 m (6 ft) high.

Common plants traditionally used for formal hedging include yew, box and the deciduous beech. *Eugenia brasiliensis* is a good choice for a thick boundary hedge (although it will grow to a height of about 4 m [13 ft], and for this purpose should always be carefully trimmed, to encourage bushing, and kept

ABOVE LEFT *Well-trimmed hedges are a feature of an English Country-style garden.*

LEFT *Pool fencing is partially obscured by planting.*

to a maximum height of around 2 m (6 ft)). *Euonymus japonica* is a useful evergreen which may be trimmed to a hedge as low as 1 m (3 ft). Both hibiscus and oleander make a good informal hedge (though bear in mind that the sap of the oleanders is poisonous). If properly trained, plumbago is another good choice for a colourful informal hedge.

Several small bushes may be planted to create a dwarf hedge, including some of the ericas (heathers), cotton lavender (*Santolina*) and even ordinary lavender (*Lavandula spica* in particular).

Conifers make good barriers, and of course will grow to a considerably greater height than the standard clipped hedge.

For a formal hedge, choose plants of approximately the same height. An informal barrier of screening shrubs, on the other hand, should be varied in species as well as height for interest.

When planting hedges or screens, be careful not to place shrubs too close together. Instant screening is seldom feasible, which is why so many people tend to over-plant. Always consider the eventual size of the species and rather fill spaces with (temporary) annuals to give colour for a season.

Precast concrete

Many homeowners who find a solid brick wall too costly opt for the precast variety. Available in a range of patterns and textures (including a type designed to look like brick), a precast concrete wall will enable you to enclose your property – although, frankly, these walls are not particularly attractive, and need abundant planting to camouflage them.

Unfortunately it is difficult to train climbers and creepers over this type of structure (they will not tolerate nails unless rawl bolts are utilized). Another solution is to place a wooden trellis in front of the wall; netting or wire is another. Or simply plant large shrubs in a generous mixed border.

Screens

Solid walls or densely planted hedges are the obvious options for boundaries; screens within the garden are usually less substantial. A trellis or lattice fence, or even a simple homemade wooden frame-

work, will effectively screen an area without blocking out light and, moreover, will allow a glimpse of what lies beyond. Planted with climbers, it will soon take on the look of an appealing foliage screen (see Hedges and plant screens, above).

A planted screen is also effective, although it will obviously take a little longer to establish.

Screens perform many functions: they will shield a service area (where rubbish bins, washing lines and so on are kept); they will create an illusion of privacy around a swimming pool or in another part of the garden, and, if well placed, prevent the wind from buffeting treasured plants.

Oval-leafed privet (Ligustrum lucidum) *has been planted between roses to create an interesting and unusual hedge alongside a tiled walkway.*

If wind is the problem, choose a screening device (a latticework fence or breeze-block structure, for example) that will allow the full force to filter through it rather than have it come up against a solid barrier and create unpleasant turbulence.

Walls

Man has been building walls since the earliest times to keep out intruders and to demarcate his boundaries – functions as valid today as they ever were.

A wall, though relatively expensive (especially if it is to encircle a large property), is nevertheless quite quickly constructed and, if combined with foliage, will add charm to the garden.

Built of stone, brick (which may be facebrick or plastered and painted) or block, walls are also a reasonably good barrier against noise and dust. They may also be built to retain earth in the garden – where there is a change in level, for example, or where a sloping site needs to be terraced.

Solid walls are particularly appropriate for the boundary of the property, while decorative breeze-blocks, which allow air to circulate and minimize turbulence, are better suited to screens within the garden (see Screens, above). Where noise is a factor, solid walls are the more sensible option: the expense is usually worth it in the long run.

If you are planning a solid structure, consider incorporating planters or niches in which statues or other decorative features can be displayed (see page 114). In a small garden, creepers will hide the hard surface while a climber such as honeysuckle, the canary creeper, the common ivy (Hedera helix) or ivy-leaved pelargoniums may be trained in a diagonal (criss-cross) pattern to add interest. If your garden is large, you may prefer to disguise the wall and, in addition, to plant a mixed border with trees behind and shrubs in front.

Another option is to incorporate espaliered trees (apple and pear are the classic choices), shrubs or climbers. Here the plant is trained against the wall to form a geometric, two-dimensional shape.

In a water garden (see pages 185-195) a wall is often suitable as a backdrop for a fountain, perhaps one with a fish or cherub spouting water into the pond.

ABOVE Ivy has been trained to create an interesting diagonal pattern on a carport wall. This formal approach is similar to the espalier technique where fruit trees are shaped flat against a wall, along wires. It is effective once plants have established themselves, but requires constant attention and regular clipping.

OPPOSITE A spurting water feature built into a bricked-in arch in a Victorian-style garden makes a charming focal point without taking up any unnecessary space. The walled effect – rather than an archway which leads somewhere – adds to the look.

A combination of materials, including brick paving, railway sleepers, ground cover, pebbles and tiles, create interest at the entrance of a modern house.

OPPOSITE
ABOVE LEFT A variety of tiles laid in an interesting geometric pattern along a walkway effectively combine with untiled squares which have been planted.

ABOVE RIGHT Brick paving abuts against concrete slabs on a leafy patio.

BELOW LEFT Brick stairs lead to a partially paved patio which incorporates concrete slabs thrown in situ.

BELOW RIGHT Moss has been allowed to creep between the gaps of concrete on an Oriental-style patio.

GARDEN FLOORS

The garden floor, which can be as varied and versatile as any floor within the house itself, is one of the most important elements of the outdoor scheme, determining both the usefulness and the attractiveness of the area as a whole.

Perhaps the most effective garden floors are those that rely on classical parterre designs, which involve a variety of plant shapes and colours – lawns, gravel and so on are arranged in such a way as to produce beautiful embroidered effects.

Of course, much will depend on the role each part of the garden has to fulfil. A patio needs a hard, level surface, while play areas for children should be soft underfoot. A pool surround will have much in common with patio and terrace, but an added pre-requisite here is safety, so it should be of a non-slip material. Ease of maintenance is a prime consider-ation in constructing the driveway, safety the most important element when it comes to pathways.

But the aesthetics are just as important, especially when choosing suitable materials. Asphalt (see be-low) is an appropriate driveway material, but is not a good choice for the patio. Similarly, brick path-ways look attractive in some settings but will not suit a wild garden (see pages 72-73).

The garden's range of hard materials should ideally complement those used in the house itself. They do not need to match, but one should work towards harmony of colour and contrast or con-sistency in texture.

Asphalt

Not very popular nowadays, asphalt (or tarmac) is nevertheless particularly useful for low-cost drive-ways and parking areas. Many people consider the material ugly, but it can easily be softened by crea-tive planting around the perimeter.

Asphalt is well suited to large properties with sweeping driveways, and is quite acceptable in one that has a Farmhouse-style garden.

Although it is a reasonably inexpensive material, it is difficult to work with: employ a specialist con-tractor to lay it for you.

Bark

Chips of bark may be used over bare parts of a bed to give a neat, clean look to what might otherwise appear a rather tatty and unkempt area. Chips are, however, not intended for walking on and should only be used in planted areas.

Brick

A popular material, brick may be laid in a variety of patterns to create a good-looking and hard-wearing surface. It is suitable for driveways, patios, pathways, steps, and is a particularly good choice for swimming pool surrounds.

Both clay and concrete bricks (sometimes called blocks) are suitable, the choice depending on the effect you want to create and on your budget. Concrete pavers are generally cheaper, but clay bricks come in a greater selection of colours and they tend to look more natural.

Sometimes old bricks may be used with effect in the garden (in a Victorian-style environment, for instance). If you have access to second-hand bricks, make quite sure that they will withstand weathering.

One of the most effective ways of visually softening an expansive brick-paved surface is to group a selection of tubs and pots on the paving. Planted with bright annuals (petunias for instance), or perennials (geraniums are a favourite) or, if there is some shade, fuchsias, they will add colour as well as variety to the area.

Another option – for an informal garden – is to scatter quick-growing seeds, alyssum (*Aurinia saxatilis*) for instance, over the brick paving and allow it to root in the cracks. The plants look pretty and will spread rapidly. Or you could leave (or even create) gaps where more established shrubs and perennials can be planted.

Concrete

Concrete is a cheap material that may be used throughout the garden. Moreover, it may be utilized on its own or in conjunction with other surfaces, including timber and brick. It is available in precast forms – as fake flagstones or sleepers, as stepping stones or ordinary slabs – or it may be cast *in situ*.

Until paving became so universally popular and affordable, concrete driveways were often laid in strips (usually with grass planted between them) leading to a garage. There was also an unfortunate tendency in some suburban areas to throw concrete over the entire backyard – a practice that did little to improve a garden's appeal.

More and more precast concrete products are coming onto the market, and although some gardeners may consider the material to be inferior, it certainly has its uses. Slabs laid in a chequerboard pattern, for instance, can form the basis for a traditional – and very attractive – herb garden. These same slabs (available in plain grey, with textured patterns in the surface, or studded with pebbles), may also be used for pathways and patios in all types of gardens. On their own, they can appear repetitive and even boring, but combined with creative planting they become an inexpensive medium for successful hard landscaping (see pages 58-59). With sensitivity, the material will blend with its natural surrounds to provide a practical garden floor that anyone would be proud of.

OPPOSITE *Concrete slabs set in a chequerboard pattern form the basis of an interesting and unusual herb garden.*

ABOVE *Simulated flagstones combine well with ground cover alongside a thatched shelter with built-in seating. The surrounding area has been covered with gravel to form a low maintenance garden space.*

Granite setts

Although not a commonly used material (similar to cobblestones, it can more often be seen as street and public pathway paving), granite setts are nevertheless suitable for garden terraces and patios.

Gravel

Sometimes laid on paths and, on flat ground, on country driveways, gravel is an inexpensive option which, more often than not, serves as a temporary arrangement. Unless the earth beneath it is well compacted, the gravel will tend to sink into the soil and become uneven. It is also impractical if you are likely to use the pathway for wheelbarrows, prams and the like.

Gravel may be used between plants, adding to a mosaic design, or between slabs, stepping stones or any other hard material.

Ground cover

The green floor of a garden need not be of grass: ground covers, of which there are a great many varieties to choose from, provide an attractive alternative. A number of species may also be planted to create a colourful carpet or dense blanket of foliage, either in place of a lawn or as part of a bed – where they will also play a valuable role suppressing weeds. Many of the varieties are also suitable for covering areas of soil around young shrubs that will fill out as they grow.

If you want to create a lawn effect without grass, consider aromatic chamomile (*Anthemis nobilis*), a hardy perennial that forms a thick, mat-like growth. Its long stems are removed by careful mowing once or twice a year.

A wild-flower meadow (see pages 72-73) is another possibility. Here flowers and various grasses cover the ground in informal fashion to produce a glorious medley of colour.

Flagstones

Although real flagstones (which are flat slabs or solid rock) are not common in all areas, a fairly wide range of simulated products is readily available. Made from reconstituted stone or concrete, they are attractive, easy to lay, and they will make practical, good-looking and hard wearing paths, patios, and even pool surrounds.

Laterite

Especially suitable for farm driveways and walkways in formal rose or herb gardens, this fine gravel and clay mixture is watered and rolled to create a good, smooth surface.

Worn railway sleepers add character to the patio of an Oriental-style garden.

Generally, a lawn will appear bigger if it is unbroken by beds, trees and pathways. If yours is a small area, let the path meander alongside a grassy edge. If, however, you have a large garden, you may welcome a tree or two to provide dappled shade during long, hot summer days.

Pebbles

Stone chips and round pebbles may be used in the same way as bark (see above) to cover bare soil and so prevent excessive loss of moisture, and to help suppress unsightly weed growth. Often, too, they are placed between paving stones or slabs to create an interesting contrast.

Rounded river-stones may also be set in concrete to produce a cobblestone effect.

Railway sleepers

The wood previously used for railway sleepers was extremely tough and will therefore wear well outdoors (for which of course the units were designed).

At one time, not so long ago, railway sleepers were a cheap material for garden use, but nowadays they are scarce and relatively expensive. Still, if you can find them, they are a good option for patios, steps, and even as a border for ground-level planters. It is preferable to separate them with a ground cover, both to enhance their attractiveness and to provide a secure grip underfoot.

Sand

This is not commonly used as a ground surface on its own, as it tends to blow away in hot, dry weather and to become messy in wet weather. It may also be difficult to maintain weed control. Sand gardens are, however, an integral part of many Japanese-style homes. In this instance, coarse sand is laid and raked into different patterns for effect.

Slate

Available in both regular and irregular shapes, slate – which is usually set on top of a concrete base – is useful for patios, paths and steps.

If this is your chosen material and yours is a formal garden, you will have to use uniform pieces (which

Lawns

Just about every garden today has at least one area of lawn. The type of grass chosen will be largely determined by its function and the look you want to create, but also by the amount of time and effort you are prepared to spend keeping it in shape. A well-manicured lawn will look lush and elegant, but it will also be time-consuming.

are not always readily obtainable) or tiles. Random 'crazy paving', on the other hand, is well suited to informal gardens, especially those planted in the old-fashioned Cottage style, and is reasonably easy to obtain. Moreover, it is a fairly easy surface to lay.

Stone

A natural garden material, stone may be used for building steps, pathways, terraces, patios and swimming pool surrounds.

Irregular pieces of cut stone are suitable for 'crazy paving'; and crushed stone may be used in much the same manner as gravel (see above). Large stones, of course, will be an essential part of any rockery or rock garden (see pages 69 and 70); and cobblestones are particularly appropriate to the Cottage style.

Simulated stone is now widely available. This is cement-based and factory moulded, regular in shape and therefore considerably simpler to lay than genuine cut stone.

One can easily soften the overall effect of a stone-paved surface, simply by allowing perennial ground covers to grow in spaces between the stones. Herbs such as thyme, creeping marjoram and pennyroyal, which release a fragrant smell when crushed underfoot, are a delight.

Tiles

Suitable for patio surfaces and pool surrounds, tiles intended for outdoor areas should always have a matt finish and be non-slip. Terrazzo, terracotta and quarry tiles are especially recommended as they will blend with the natural environment in terms of both texture and colour.

Outdoor tiles are laid in exactly the same way as the indoor type: on a smoothly screeded concrete surface and then grouted.

Timber

The most common decking material, and suitable for many parts of the garden. Choose hard woods (meranti, afrormosia, Philippine mahogany or teak) and treat for longevity. Pine is not an appropriate timber for garden construction.

A major advantage of timber decking is that it enables homeowners on steeply sloping plots to establish a useful flat surface without excavation, retaining walls and so on. In this situation, it is often the most practical material available.

Nicely rounded slices of tree-trunk make attractive stepping stones. Place them in ground cover (it is generally tricky to keep lawn looking trim around the circular pieces). Although they do tend to become slippery, they can also be used for rustic garden steps, and even for a patio or driveway. If laid over a reasonably wide area ensure that the finish is slightly uneven. This will provide a grip for car wheels and make it less treacherous in wet weather.

Non-slip tiles are a practical option in outdoor areas, especially in high-rainfall regions.

A reed ceiling provides shelter from the sun on a small patio.

OPPOSITE

ABOVE LEFT *Striped shadecloth has been attached to a gum pole pergola constructed over an attractive koi pond.*

ABOVE RIGHT *Reeds provide welcome shade from the sun on a Mediterreanean-style patio.*

BELOW LEFT *A shadecloth-covered pergola gives shelter from the sun on an elaborate outdoor entertaining area.*

BELOW RIGHT *A pretty Victorian-style porch is perfect for alfresco eating.*

SHELTER

There are a great many options for providing shelter within the garden, ranging from verandahs and covered pergolas on patios adjacent to the house, to more elaborate structures like gazebos and summerhouses.

While function determines the location of the shelter, style will influence the type of protection or 'ceiling' chosen. If you have a tennis court, the chances are you will want a summerhouse in which players and guests can sit on hot, sunny days. A gazebo will be best suited to a Victorian-style house and garden, while a thatched cabin would look more appropriate in a farmhouse environment.

If you are planning a patio for entertaining, this too may require some kind of protective cover.

Even if your garden has not been planned to conform to a particular style, it is important that a garden shelter relates comfortably to the house itself. A wooden pergola tacked onto the side of a severe, symmetrical, Georgian-style building will look rather odd, while the same structure, planted with creepers and climbers, would immediately add to the charm of a country cottage or farmhouse.

Of course the *amount* of protection you require is also a major factor. The pergola will provide shade from the sun and may shield you from some of the wind, but it will not be proof against rain. For this, a more permanent type of roof will be needed.

The arbour

The traditional arbour was a simple, semi-enclosed structure designed to give some shelter from the elements and to introduce a touch of intimacy and seclusion into a garden. Constructed principally as a support for plants, it also housed a seat of some sort and provided an inviting, sun-dappled little retreat. Although invariably smothered with plants, the basic structure remained partially open to the sky – a feature sometimes overlooked in the modern version of the arbour.

Arbours in ancient Egypt appear to have been practical rather than decorative, erected for the cultivation of grape vines. The Romans also constructed arbours, although these were grander structures, sometimes built on stone columns and with open lattice roofs. By the mid-16th century, the arbour formed a familiar part of the English garden and was, again, a simple arrangement, often assembled from willow or juniper stems (rather like the Victorian bower) and, once planted with rosemary, box or

another of the favoured plants of the day, became a living structure. The Victorians, on the other hand, favoured relatively open, wirework arbours that were often planted with roses.

The modern 'arbour' is closer in character to a pergola, even though a more traditional design can be easily erected. A simple but charming result can be attained by building an arch and planting over and around on three sides to create (in terms of the dictionary definition) 'a shady retreat with sides and roof of trees or climbing plants'.

Perhaps the most ambitious type is the topiary arbour, for which the dense foliage of an evergreen tree is carefully clipped and hollowed out to create a living shelter around a seat.

A huge number of plants are suited to arbours, among them such sweet-smelling climbers as jasmine and honeysuckle. Other possibilities include wisteria, which, although it is deciduous, will add a sensational splash of colour to the garden when it flowers; the self-clinging, silver-veined creeper *Parthenocissus henryana* or clematis, which does better in colder climates.

Arbours are commonly sited at the end of a path or in a reasonably secluded corner of the garden, although there is nothing to prevent you incorporating one into a patio area close to the house. At Sissinghurst, in England, the white garden (see page 67) features a typical Victorian arbour, smothered in white roses and positioned centrally at the point where four paths converge.

Awnings

Adjustable awnings are ideal for patios where there is a need for both sun and shade. These are available as lightweight aluminium louvres or in canvas. The colour should be in keeping with the house and garden (see pages 75-83).

An attractive shadecloth awning gives welcome protection from the sun.

Conservatories

Though the conservatory is usually considered a part of the house, its origins can in fact be traced to 17th century orangeries built alongside houses (and mansions) to give protection to plants.

By the mid-19th century, the English had developed cheaper and better quality glass as well as iron glazing-bars to support it. As a result, elaborate conservatories and sophisticated greenhouses became familiar attachments to Victorian homes. Here, all types of exotic plants were tended until they could either be transferred into the garden or displayed within the house.

Popular types of modern conservatory include glass extensions and custom-made rooms with glass walls. Even though the former tend to get rather hot in summer, they do have the appealing effect of bringing the garden indoors.

The gazebo

This time-honoured structure (see page 153) is a perfect means of shelter for the large garden, especially that which inclines towards the Victorian style. Essentially an outdoor room with a view, a gazebo (sometimes called a pavilion) was often raised – on a terrace, for instance – to take in a vista beyond the property. Traditionally it was a delightful little building, often constructed from wood but sometimes from stone or brick, and had a steeply-pitched roof of either shingle, slate or thatch (depending on the style of the house). It had both doors and windows and was either square or octagonal in shape.

The renowned gardener Gertrude Jekyll (see page 203), had a celebrated gazebo in her garden at Munstead Wood, a retreat that was dubbed 'the thunder house' because it was here that she would sit and watch the summer storms that swept over the landscape. Designed by her partner, Sir Edwin Luytens

A traditional Victorian-style conservatory helps bring the garden into the house.

(see page 204), it was described as 'a plain little building' that matched the local stone used in the house and elsewhere and enabled Miss Jekyll to see over the fields and beyond to the distant hills.

If sited some distance from the house, the style of a gazebo can be as whimsical as you choose. However, it is still preferable to have some kind of visual link between the two. Consider using the same tiles or sheeting for the roof, or perhaps mirror pillars to support a verandah.

When planting beside a gazebo, it is important to ensure that vigorous creepers, such as bougainvillaea, which thrives in warm climates, have adequate support. Alternatively, opt for a lighter plant – perhaps the sweetly scented Chilean jasmine (*Mandevilla laxa*) or pink flowering M. *splendens* (both of which are best suited to temperate parts), or the semi-hardy canary creeper which bears clusters of bright yellow flowers in late summer and autumn. Or you could plant an annual climber – Black-eyed Susan (*Thunbergia alata*), for example – which will grow quickly to provide additional screening in summer but will give the structure maximum exposure to sunlight in the cold winter months.

Pergolas

The pergola has a history dating back at least to Roman times (as murals at Pompeii show). Originally developed to give some shelter from the hot Mediterranean summer sun (making them an obvious feature in gardens created in this style), they are nowadays often built for purely decorative purposes in cooler climates.

A pergola (the Latin word *pergula* means a projecting roof or eave) is an ideal frame for climbing plants (see Plant ceilings, below), but may also be 'roofed' with wooden slats, shadecloth (see page 204) which is now available in a selection of colours or an awning of some type (see Awnings, above). The structure can be freestanding or attached to the house. It is often constructed over a patio or carport to give shade, but may be erected to form a covered walkway in the garden or even over a driveway. In fact, Sir Edwin Lutyens, who may be regarded as the master of the pergola, often used it to link house and garden.

When it comes to size, it all depends on your personal needs and preferences. There are no hard and fast rules: pictures of some Renaissance gardens show grand pergolas long enough to shade horse and rider during their daily gallop.

Materials will be determined largely by the style of the house and garden. Uprights may be stone, brick, cut timber or poles, even trellis panelling, while cross-pieces overhead will almost always be of wood of some kind.

ABOVE *A charming Victorian gazebo provides an inviting shady retreat on hot summer days.*

OPPOSITE *A leafy glade where trees provide shade is a good place to site table and chairs.*

Hooped timber arches – which would have to be built by a skilled carpenter – will make a stunning pergola, especially if galvanized wire or something similar is stretched along the top to carry climbing plants, and to create a tunnel of soft foliage. Alternatively, consider a classical English pergola with hoops of iron set across a wide walkway.

If gum poles are your preference, choose ones that have been given a tanalith treatment. Do not use creosote: this black, tar-like substance is toxic to both plants and animals, and if the structure is covered with shadecloth, it will eventually rot this too.

The range of pergola plants is vast and varied and, once again, choice will depend largely on the surrounding environment. Rambling roses, for instance, are an obvious option for a Victorian or English Country garden (see pages 37-43), while crimson-hued bougainvillea is a must for the Mediterranean-style exterior (see pages 45-47).

Plant ceilings

One of the most effective ways to create atmosphere in a garden is to allow creepers and climbers to form a natural plant canopy over pergolas, archways and other structures.

Any reasonably light material will serve as a framework: timber, metal, even rope or chain hung between uprights to form swags.

Trees, too, will of course give shade, and some may even be planted so that they intertwine, forming a continuous line and an attractive plant ceiling.

While a plant ceiling will not provide shelter from the rain or from hail and snow, it will protect you from the sun and, when well established, usually from the wind too. Providing the climate is right, various climbers such as the Zimbabwe climber (*Podranea brycei*), golden shower (*Pyrostegia venusta*) and a wide selection of bougainvillaea will also create a riot of colour in summer as well as afford welcome protection. The evergreen Chinese jasmine (*Jasminum polyanthum*) will add a beautiful fragrance when planted up the sides of a pergola or gazebo, as will the lovely lilac-flowering wisteria (W. *sinensis*) – which is deciduous – and various honeysuckles, most of which are also evergreen.

The choice will of course depend on whether you want protection all year round or whether you need to let some sunlight into the area in the colder winter months. A dense ceiling of creepers over a patio attached to the house will serve as a cool, leafy retreat in summer, but will tend to make the house cold in winter. Here, it would be more sensible to opt for deciduous plants – Virginia creeper (*Parthenocissus quinquefolia*), for example (although this is a self-clinging species akin to ivy, and this may make maintenance of the structure a problem), or an ornamental or fruiting grape vine.

The summerhouse

Perhaps more accurately termed a 'garden house', this is a covered retreat, similar to (and sometimes confused with) the gazebo and pavilion, where there is sufficient space to relax and spend time out of the hot summer sun.

However, unlike the ornate gazebo, the summerhouse is a simple, often partially open-sided building which sometimes features a thatched roof. The traditional Victorian structure was large enough to seat eight or ten people, for it was here that the family would invariably 'take tea' in the summer months. The ultimate 19th-century design was mounted on a turntable base which could be rotated, so providing its occupants with a variety of views.

Well sited, a modern summerhouse can serve as the venue for a range of activities – weekend luncheons, dinners and so on – and may be particularly effective when established beside the swimming pool. It may also double as a children's playhouse.

Umbrellas

While ordinary garden umbrellas will provide some protection from the sun, large, canvas, market-style models are an even better option. Thatch umbrellas will provide a more permanent shelter.

Verandahs

A covered verandah offers shade from the sun and shelter from the wind and rain, and because it is a part of the structure of the house itself, it will often become the family's outdoor room.

The type and style of verandah chosen will determine the materials used in its construction. A traditional Cape Dutch stoep running the length of the house will be built of bricks and mortar, with a concrete surface that is usually tiled. A Victorian-style verandah, on the other hand, will feature decorative wrought-ironwork, wooden lattice or carpenter's lace.

Wood – planed timber or gum poles for instance – is a particularly popular choice for the modern verandah, or deck.

OPPOSITE *Vines flourish over a backyard pergola, which covers a patio used primarily for tending pot plants.*

BELOW *A covered, but open-sided, modern patio is elegantly furnished for casual entertaining.*

An attractive garden lamp illuminates plants beside a
swimming pool.

OPPOSITE
ABOVE LEFT   A charming water feature is illuminated by
concealed lighting.

ABOVE RIGHT   Carefully positioned lights between classic
columns add architectural interest to the house, while
modern lamps illuminate the pool and patio area at night.
Design: André Hodgskin.

BELOW LEFT   A built-in barbecue area is floodlit, with
garden candles adding to the atmosphere.

BELOW RIGHT   Concealed uplighters create mood in a
sloping garden.

LIGHTING

Garden lighting has an important place in the decorative scheme, adding a further dimension to the outdoor area. A few strategically placed fittings will immediately bring the garden alive, accentuating the shapes and forms of plants, lending charm and character to patios, poolsides, barbecue areas, transforming even a mediocre garden into a magical fairyland at night.

Outdoor lighting also has its practical value of course. On the patio, it enables you to entertain at night in attractively atmospheric surrounds. And it is also important from both a security and a safety point of view, illuminating dark areas where intruders could lurk unseen, as well as features – pathways and steps, for example – that could pose a hazard in the dark. If there are large rocks in unexpected places, these too should be highlighted in some way. For safety reasons pool areas should always be properly lit, preferably with underwater lighting as well as floodlights or spots.

Other entertainment and activity areas – tennis court, barbecue and so on – also need some form of permanent lighting, as does the entrance to your property, the front door and its surrounds, and the garage. Here, an automatic system, activated when the natural light fades, is a particularly good option. These systems operate either within a certain distance of an electrically powered control box, or from a mechanism in the light fitting itself. The latter option is considerably cheaper, but unfortunately does not have a very long lifespan and will need to be replaced from time to time.

Light fittings attached to the house are usually part of the internal electrical arrangement; those in the garden may be on a separate circuit. And, just as all electrical installations in the house must be carried out by a licensed electrician, so too must those in the garden. If your property is large, or if you are fitting a borehole or swimming pool pump, he may have to alter the single-phase system to a three-phase one (these additional amenities draw a lot more power than the 15 kva – kilovolt amps – provided by the standard power source).

The electrician will also have to use suitable waterproof cabling (which he will bury underground) and ensure that there is earth leakage. Make absolutely certain you know where all the cables are located, and pass this information on to anyone else working in the garden: one has to be very careful to avoid the accidental severing of underground wiring.

Type

Exterior lighting may either be direct, casting a single beam, or evenly spread, casting a general glow over the outdoor area. Some forms of lighting are a lot more decorative than functional, giving very little useful illumination.

Direct Spotlights cast a direct shaft of light in a particular direction. This may be for practical reasons – to light up that part of the garden around the front door, for instance – or it may be designed to emphasize a particular element of the garden. Focal points include statues and sculptures, garden benches, and special plant features, although spots are also commonly used within a garden bed (as uplighters).

Generally speaking, reflected illumination is the more attractive. Aim to bounce direct light off walls or plants, or plan direct lighting so that there is some diffusion of the beam – by concealing it in foliage, for example, or behind a tree. This will produce a gentler, prettier effect.

General Overall general lighting is difficult to achieve in the garden unless a fair number of fittings are positioned at strategic points. But this rarely presents a problem, as it is far more effective to create pools of light within the garden itself and to limit general lighting to limited spaces, like patio and pool area. Here, lamps and wall-mounted fittings will usually be sufficient.

Bollard lights are well suited to driveways and pathways, and a series of these set along the edges will give good general illumination.

Although floodlights technically fall within the category of direct lighting, they are powerful enough to wash a wide area with illumination, so creating a 'general' lighting effect.

Decorative uplighters illuminate a patio. Additional general lighting is provided from within the house.

Decorative Many types of lighting are decorative as well as practical – uplighters will dramatize leaf shapes, highlighting the foliage, while lamps will cast a moody glow over a wider area.

Some light fittings, including period-style free-standing lamps, wall-mounted carriage lamps and moulded Japanese lamps are attractive features in themselves.

Coloured fairy lights are also decorative, of course, but more suited to festivities than permanent garden lighting. Strung around an entertainment patio or barbecue area, or over the branches of large trees, they will help create a party atmosphere. However, if you are going to install permanent coloured lights, first consider the effect different colours will have on foliage. For instance, blue light should generally be avoided as it is cold and will give an unnatural look to plants. Green and amber are probably the best choices for most gardens.

Fittings

A wide selection of lights and lamps are suitable for the garden and patio. Intended for exposure to rain, the units are sealed for protection. Those to be used in flower beds often incorporate plastic spikes to help fix them firmly into the ground.

Low-voltage illumination is especially useful if you want to create mood lighting in the outdoor area, particulary on patios.

The style of light fitting chosen is important only, of course, if it is to be visible. An old Victorian street lamp will look charming at the entrance to a house built in this period; similarly, concrete Japanese lamps will enhance a garden planned in the genre.

However, many fittings are better concealed, so that they create mood rather than simply introduce bright shafts of light.

Modern garden lamps are in keeping with the style of an oversized thatched umbrella, while the pool itself has underwater lighting.

Candles Although candles fall in the category of temporary lighting, they have their uses in the garden. Ordinary ones may be used on an outdoor table to create atmosphere during alfresco eating, or you may prefer special, slow-burning garden ones mounted on sticks set in the ground. More sophisticated bamboo flares are also available.

For parties and special events, place candles in brown paper packets half filled with sand. They will glow beautifully and the packet will prevent the wind from extinguishing the flames.

Floating candles are another charming option for festive occasions. These may be placed in water-filled bowls on the table, or perhaps on the surface of a pond or even of the swimming pool.

Floodlights These intensely bright lights are used to 'flood' large areas with light. But, since a little illumination goes a long way in the garden, they are not widely used except on very large properties where security is a vital factor. If you have a tennis court, however, it will of course need to be floodlit if you are to use it at night.

Lamps A wide range of freestanding lamps are available for wall-mounting, for the tops of pillars, and for fitting on sturdy posts. They are useful for many outdoor areas where illumination is essential, including the entrance to a driveway, outside the front door, and alongside a pathway or long drive. They are particularly practical for patios and other entertainment areas.

For a covered verandah, an ordinary lamp may be permanently located on a table, provided it is kept away from the open and from the moisture that can drift in. Here the choice of shade is important, as anything too flimsy will easily be damaged by harsh sunlight. The lamp itself should also be sturdy enough to withstand wind.

Hand-held gas lamps are not particularly pretty, but they are useful in areas which do not have permanent lighting. They are also a sensible solution if you have not yet installed your outdoor system.

Lanterns Hanging lanterns may be used on the patio in addition to other more permanent lighting. There are various types on the market, including those fuelled with paraffin and oil. Inexpensive candle lamps are also available. Hurricane lamps, designed to withstand high-velocity winds, can be useful and they look good in a Victorian-style garden.

Pool lighting Most pools and spas that have underwater lighting are so equipped when they are installed or constructed. This kind of illumination looks attractive and, moreover, has its relevance in terms of safety (among other things they enable you to keep an eye on the swimmers, and to act effectively should anyone get into difficulty).

If a pool does not have underwater lighting, it is important to ensure that the area is well lit with spotlights, lamps or by a floodlight. Remember that paving can become slippery when wet, which is a particular hazard at night.

Concealed lighting in flowerbeds dramatizes leaf shapes and highlights foliage.

In addition to underwater and specific lighting, consider illuminating areas of the surrounding garden for effect, especially if you like to entertain guests by the pool in the evening.

Spotlights These may be mounted on the external walls of the house or grouped within the branches of a large tree, the intensity of their light depending largely on where they are located.

Spotlights are useful and practical on barbecue patios and for other kinds of alfresco eating, where they can be positioned to throw a pool of light over the surface of the table, and are ideal as accent lighting, drawing attention to statuary and other ornamental garden features. They are particularly effective near water, which will sparkle and shimmer in the golden glow.

If the patio is used for specific activities at night – reading, for example – spotlights are the most sensible option, fulfilling the same function as any other localized indoor task lighting.

Uplighters Used for both general and direct lighting, uplighters are a particularly useful device for creating effect within a large bed planted with shrubs and perennials, and for illuminating the foliage of trees (but it is sensible to take the trouble to place the fittings behind the trunk to create an interesting silhouette effect).

Uplighters may also be used in flowerbeds or between shrubs alongside a driveway or path to give a diffused light, bright enough to guide you on your way home after dark.

Wall-mounted lights There is a reasonably wide choice of lights manufactured for use on patios and external walls. These range from plain glass units to attractive carriage lamps. Wall-mounted lights, fitted low down, are also useful for illuminating steps.

A small patio relies on light from the house and underwater lighting in the tiny plunge pool.

Ferns have been allowed to grow through the paving to soften the lines of a classical pot.

OPPOSITE

ABOVE LEFT A *delightful circular fish-pond with two chimney pots adding a special finishing touch.*

ABOVE RIGHT A *simple precast concrete bird-bath is the focal point in a flowerbed.*

BELOW LEFT A *trompe l'oeil by James Hemphill adds perspective to an otherwise uninspiring garden view.*

BELOW RIGHT An *elegant little statue set in a formal lily-pond is reflected in the water.*

FINISHING TOUCHES

Just as flowers, ornaments, sculptures and other collectable items add those final touches to the interior of a house, so it is with the exterior spaces of your home, where statuary, topiary, a selection of well-chosen containers, perhaps a sundial, a bird-bath, a fountain, will add character. Seating, too, can inject an element of originality, while lighting, imaginatively planned, will give the garden a distinctive night-time personality.

On the more lavish property, the whimsical appeal of a folly will provide a talking point. Or you might consider either treillage (see page 204) or a painted *trompe l'oeil*, which will add a fascinating dimension to what might otherwise be an ordinary, even a dull space. To introduce a hint of illusory charm, a boundary wall can be effectively decorated with stencilled flowers or, for those with more artistic talents, a realistic landscape of fields, trees or even painted topiary bushes. If you have a patio which is covered by a lush vine in summer, but which becomes bare and desolate in winter, think about a little painted greenery (perhaps with a few butterflies and bees) to introduce a seasonal colour – and just a bit of wit – to the scene.

Benches and seats

Outdoor seating has an essentially practical purpose (see pages 159-165), but it can also be a beautifully decorative and distinctive feature, enhancing the attractiveness of the garden as a whole, inviting one to sit, relax, and generally to absorb the universal pleasures of nature in quietness.

It is important that any bench or seat placed in the garden, should look as if it is *meant* to be there (even temporary seating should suggest permanence). It should also be thoughtfully positioned to take advantage of the best aspect or view, and to complement the overall garden plan.

The type of seating chosen should, like all other forms of ornamentation, blend with the other materials used in the garden. The style, too, should be in keeping with the general design. For example, a precast concrete bench, left to collect mossy growth in cracks and crevices, will enhance most informal gardens, while an elaborate, filigree cast-iron design will look well in an outdoor space created in the Victorian genre, though it would be quite out of place in a simple Japanese garden and in most Mediterranean-style exteriors.

Containers

Tubs, pots, barrels and window boxes planted with lush foliage, or colourful annuals or perennials, will brighten up dull, unattractive corners and bare spots; placed on either side of the front door, they serve to make an opening statement; along a verandah, they will add life and help create atmosphere; and sensitively arranged on the patio, will have a softening effect and lend extra colour and texture to the area. If the container itself is appealing, it may itself provide a striking focal point.

The type and colour of a container must of course be compatible with its surrounds. For instance, while terracotta pots will be appropriate to most gardens, especially those of the Mediterranean type, the ornately moulded variety will not be well suited to a simple Japanese-style exterior.

And the container must be compatible with its contents: consider colour, shape and the eventual size and height of the plants you intend to pot. Use a decent potting soil (even if you are transplanting directly from a bag), and ensure there is sufficient drainage for the species you select.

There are many plants which thrive in containers (though some of them need less care than others), among them fuchsias, begonias, petunias and geraniums. The last-named, which belong to the *Pelargonium* family, originated in the western Cape region of South Africa, and are now found in window boxes and pots all over the world.

Choice of container is largely a personal matter. There are numerous concrete, terracotta and fibrecement varieties available in many shapes and patterns, both simple and elaborate, to suit every taste. On the market, too, are many ceramic pots, some of which are mass produced, others handcrafted; and of course an abundance of plastic pots, both standing and designed (in imitation of the Victorian basket) for hanging.

African clay pots make excellent receptacles for plants, but they are porous and will eventually deteriorate from exposure to constant moisture.

If your preference is for the more unusual, look around for receptacles which can be 'recycled' — adapted for garden purposes. Old troughs, cisterns

and sinks make surprisingly effective containers, particularly for succulents and alpine plants. Used wooden wine barrels are a popular choice, well suited to the Cape Dutch or Farmhouse look; obsolete chimney pots, tin watering cans no longer in use, old ball-and-claw baths and worn wheelbarrows, all will introduce an attractively whimsical element into your garden.

While containers are often at their most effective when grouped together, it is not wise to mix the different styles: to do so would produce an unsettling discordance.

A variety of containers, all painted white, are grouped for effect at one end of a swimming pool.

Follies

The idea of a costly but useless, often monumental, folly in the garden is one that enjoyed its heyday in 18th-century Britain, when everything from caves to pyramids and ruined buildings could be found in the larger private gardens. However, 'temples' (designed for contemplation rather than prayer) and simulated ruins were also popular among the aristocracy a century earlier, when landscape designers aimed to contrive an atmosphere of poignant melancholy with these outrageous flights of fancy.

During the latter part of the 19th century, follies (and temples for that matter) again became popular, although this time in a more lighthearted and creative way. While reproductions of Classical models remained fashionable enough, Victorian designers and wealthy landowners did their utmost to introduce some originality, forfeiting the historical symbolism for visual witticism on a grand scale.

Today, it is only the more affluent homeowner who can even consider a folly of the orthodox kind. But the idea can be adapted for more modest circumstances. Here, fragments rather than grand edifices create the desired impression: a broken capital from a Classical-style column (the type freely available from concrete works) stuck in the ground and covered with ivy, for example, will suggest a folly. Or, if you are a handyman with some bricklaying experience, you could build a modern folly – a ruin in the best tradition – with scraps salvaged from a demolition yard. Plant the surrounding area with wild flowers, without worrying too much about weeds. As mentioned, though, such a feature would only be appropriate on the larger property.

Lamps and lanterns

Garden lighting has practical value (see pages 105-109), but lamps and lanterns can of course be highly decorative as well. Moreover, they will also enhance the style you wish to create. Stone lanterns will fit the Japanese theme; hurricane lamps are perfect for the Victorian-style patio.

If your permanent lighting is strictly functional, take advantage of decorative portable units – especially on special occasions.

Ornaments

Ornamentation is just as important outside the house as it is inside, although of course fewer individual items will be displayed. The selection of garden ornaments ranges from statues of all sizes and styles, sculptures and sundials to urns, birdcages and wall plaques.

The need for good taste cannot be stressed strongly enough when it comes to garden ornamentation: too much of what is available will look messy, vulgar, ostentatious, or otherwise at odds with the style of the house.

A series of pillars, rescued when Cullinan House was demolished, have been used to create a unique folly and restful retreat at St Margaret's, an historic home in Parktown, Johannesburg, South Africa.

It is also important to choose the right spot for an ornamental feature. A sundial or concrete bird-bath, for example, will successfully become the focal point if placed at the end of a formal walkway or where several paths meet. Remember that some objects will look better grouped than individually and randomly placed.

Statuary Garden statues certainly draw the attention, especially if they are large and prominently positioned, but few properties can comfortably accommodate them (indeed, one body of opinion would have statuary of any kind restricted to public parks and stately properties). Garden gnomes, so popular in certain types of suburban area, are now almost universally derided.

Nevertheless, scaled-down sculpture of some artistic merit can be effective if well placed, with shrubs and flowers sympathetically established around it, even partially hiding it. Precast statues in classical styles are widely available.

Many artists and craftsmen are turning out original works (in a wide assortment of materials, including stone, wood, metal and clay) that will enhance and lend distinction to even the smallest garden.

Urns and vases Other smaller ornaments, including elegant urns (painted concrete can be most effective) and vases, may be placed on pedestal or plinth. While these were traditionally used on the tops of pillars flanking an exterior staircase, they look just as attractive at each end of a wall, on the patio or in among foliage plants. Exercise restraint when planting them, ensuring that leaves and flowers do not engulf the receptacle.

Unusual statuary and a selection of attractive pots give character to the garden.

Sundials Even though they no longer have practical use, sundials are a popular ornament, even for modern surrounds – in a formal rose or herb garden, for instance. Traditional instruments are commonly reproduced, although often to a smaller scale.

The basic elements of a sundial are the supporting pedestal, the dial itself, and a triangular plate or gnomon. The way these are assembled, however, varies from the reasonably ordinary, set on a brick pillar, to the elaborate, which usually incorporates an ornate sculptured base and a brass dial.

To be visually effective, the sundial should – even if you never use it to tell the time – be placed in an open spot, free from shadows.

Wall-mounted objects Certain of these ornamental items – including some types of sundial, plaques, panels and so on – may also be wall-mounted. Mounted spouting fountains are ideal for the smaller patio or courtyard.

An alternative to relief decoration is to incorporate recessed niches and alcoves in a new wall and to place an urn or statue inside.

Topiary

An ancient art (it goes back to the Romans), topiary is not widely practised today. However, it is an ornamental form worth considering if you have the time and the space and are prepared to put the

BELOW LEFT *An ornamental sundial adds interest to a pretty Cottage garden.*

BELOW *Water spurts from a wall-mounted fish fountain into a bowl before trickling into the fish-pond.*

effort into clipping and training plants into specific shapes. Only certain species are suitable, and it takes years and years to achieve the desired effect, but, with patience, just about any shape may be achieved with topiary – geometric, round or oval forms, even animals and birds.

Fairly simple topiary features may literally be sculpted, by clipping. More complicated outlines will require a wire framework around which the plant is trained. When choosing a design, consider the maintenance factor: features with numerous curved features will be more time-consuming than those with straight sides. Knot gardens, which had their heyday in the 16th century, are also created by pinching out shoots and clipping plants into decorative hedges.

(*Buxus sempervirens*), yew (*Taxas baccata*) and privet (*Ligustrum japonicum*) are traditional favourites for topiary, though certain shrubby honeysuckle plants (*Lonicera nitida*, for instance), holly (*Ilex* spp.) and the sweet bay (*Laurus nobilis*), which is a particularly easy-to-grow evergreen tree, are just as suitable.

Individual plants may be used, or you can convert an existing hedge, clipping the top portion and retaining the lower bushes as a plinth.

Water features

The classic water garden – which incorporates larger pools, streams, waterfalls and so on – tends to be an expansive and elaborate affair (see pages 185-189). Smaller decorative water features, however, may be introduced in isolation adding charm to the tiniest garden or patio area. These include precast fountains, spurting heads and bird-baths, all of which, but especially those in courtyards and on secluded patios, will add character and charm to the outdoor area.

Where there is borehole water, a well may be built for both practical purposes and as an attractive feature in itself. Alternatively, consider an ornamental wishing well, which, like many other decorative elements, may either be located in a prominently visible position – where two paths intersect or in a formal rose garden, for example – or in a secluded part of the garden.

OPPOSITE

ABOVE   A tree clipped into a flat-topped umbrella shape shades a life-sized statue.

BELOW LEFT   An elaborate figured bird-bath placed to form the focal point in a corner of the garden.

BELOW RIGHT   A textured precast bird-bath painted to resemble the colour of wood.

ABOVE LEFT   An attractive arched bridge leads to a well-camouflaged outdoor wine cellar.

ABOVE   A terracotta pot makes an unusual fish-pond.

LEFT   A life-sized statue adds interest to a water garden.

PART THREE

FEATURES FOR ALL SEASONS

Designing, re-designing or simply improving the garden and other outdoor areas of the property can be a stimulating challenge, that will bring pleasure to the whole family. You may be faced with a barren landscape devoid of plants, or perhaps you have inherited an unkempt jungle of weeds. Or the garden may incorporate a number of features and plants that are well worth retaining as the basis for a new-look outdoor arrangement. The following pages will help you assess what you have, and offer some ideas on ways to enhance your assets. Here, we discuss each of the main ingredients of the garden and its environs, from the external gates and doors to patios, swimming pools and gazebos. With the basic principles we considered in the earlier chapters, you will now be able to plan and create such diverse areas as a cool and shady water garden, a special place for children to play and a practical yet pretty kitchen garden.

Dramatic architectural detail frames a bright turquoise swimming pool. Custom-made furniture, crafted from wood and concrete, completes the effect.

The entrance to a row of townhouses, designed by architect John Rushmere, is in keeping with the unusual style of the facebrick development.

OPPOSITE   *An attractive brick paved driveway is a practical and low-maintenance option. An abundance of plants, in pots and in adjacent flowerbeds, give the entrance a soothing quality.*

ENTRANCES

First impressions count for a lot, so it is important to ensure that the outside of the house, and the entrance in particular, will do justice to the interior, and that there is stylistic harmony between the two areas.

The basic approach one takes will depend mainly on the size of the property and where it is located. In a city suburb, where the average plot is around the 500-m² (600 sq yds) mark, the house will be plainly visible from the street and you will need to pay special attention to the security aspects as well as the aesthetics. A stately manor house, or a rambling country homestead, will have an entirely different kind of entrance, as will a more extensive city property. Here it will be the area around the main gate that first draws the attention, and thereafter the stretch between the entrance and front door.

Many smaller properties have garages that front onto the street, so their doors as well as the access point into the house must always be considered. Garage doors are in their nature large and plainly functional, and care should therefore be taken that they do not dominate the exterior scheme. To reduce their prominence, they should either be painted the same colour as an adjacent wall or matched with the front door.

And then, of course, planting will have to complement the character of the house and its entrance. The options here are many and various: you could, for example, choose a symmetrical, ordered design, with balanced flowerbeds and a neat pathway, or (if the property slopes) steps leading to the front door which is, in turn, enhanced by pots or tubs strategically placed on either side. If the house has a touch of quaintness about it, you could contrive a Cottage-style scheme, with the entire approach filled with colourful flowers and herbs (see pages 33-35); or, if your preference is for the Japanese approach, you could incorporate a curved stepping stone path set in gravel. A Cape Dutch homestead will traditionally feature an oak-lined driveway perhaps with hydrangeas planted along the front of the verandah.

BOUNDARY DOORS AND GATES

Almost every property has at least one gate or door leading in from the road: even if the area directly in front of the house is left unfenced, a wall or hedge frequently encloses a section behind the building to provide the privacy and security that is so important nowadays.

Boundary doorways and gates are as varied in type and style as the fences and walls that enclose a property (see pages 85-88). Designs, though, should complement the architecture of the house, either by duplicating certain features, or simply by 'framing' the house in a sympathetic way.

Choose materials that are consistent with those used elsewhere in the garden. Timber and metal are the two most common; ironwork has been popular for centuries and may be successfully combined with wooden fencing or hedges; wooden gates generally create a more modest impression, but are suitable in most situations.

Where a high wall has been built, a solid wooden door may be your best option: it will look neat, give total privacy, and offer the kind of security that most pretty garden gates lack. It can, for instance, be fitted with a bell and a two-way communication system, or a spy glass, or even a unit that will enable you to view visitors on a small television-type screen. If you have electronically operated metal gates at the entrance to the driveway, consider a second, smaller, wrought-iron pedestrian gate (of the same type) for both convenience and visual appeal. This, too, may be fitted with an intercom.

Where security is not the major factor, it is best to be guided by the style of the house and garden: an elaborate cast-iron gate will suit a Victorian town-house, while a simple wooden design, one that allows a view of the garden, will be more appropriate to the country Cottage or Farmhouse-style property.

OPPOSITE *An interesting medley of colours decorates a house designed by Clara da Cruz Almeida. Colours co-ordinated by Heber van Zyl.*

RIGHT *White roses creep over an arched gateway situated on the boundary of a suburban home.*

THE DRIVEWAY

Wherever a property is large enough to accommodate vehicular traffic, a driveway of some kind will be necessary. Depending on the general layout and the space available, this may lead right up to the front door, to an adjacent garage, or on some older suburban plots to the rear of the house.

Any driveway must of course be wide enough for cars, and there must be enough space for the occupants to open and shut doors on both sides, and long enough to accommodate the opening and closing of entrance gates and garage doors. If the drive leads directly into the garage, and does not incorporate an additional parking area or forecourt, try to ensure there is sufficient room to turn.

In the past many suburban plots incorporated the garage at the back, the driveway running down the side of the house (and often surfaced with two long strips of concrete, cast *in situ*). Today, though, most garages are sited at the front, and many have direct access to the interior. The driveway now takes up a lot less space − but, it must be well designed: it remains an important element in the garden plan.

The most popular driveway materials are concrete and clay brick, which are visually pleasing and hardwearing, and may be laid in a wide variety of attractive patterns. Asphalt is another, less expensive choice and one that can be surprisingly attractive, especially when edged with a contrasting brick. It should, however, be laid by professionals. Concrete is still an option, though it is susceptible to oil stains and does tend to crack.

A driveway leading into a larger property can be a grandly imposing affair, but take care that the materials do not overwhelm. Even brick, which again is the most common choice, can look starkly severe if it is not softened by imaginative perimeter planting − pots and tubs filled with colourful flowers, for example, or perhaps a pond or fountain (see pages 187 and 189). If space permits, a central feature often works particularly well.

OPPOSITE   *An attractive brick paved driveway, softened by flower beds and planters around the perimeter.*

RIGHT   *Water cascades over rocks and into a series of ponds which flood the driveway, creating what appears to be a natural water feature. Landscaping: Patrick Watson.*

THE FRONT DOOR

The style and character of your home will determine the type of its front door. One also has a choice when it comes to prominence: the door can be modestly inauspicious, or a feature in itself; it may incorporate a generous overhang or a porch that will offer shelter to those about to enter, or it may open directly to the outside.

The range of door types available is fairly extensive: solid, glazed, panelled; of timber, aluminium or other kinds of metal; or custom-made to architects' specification. While most are hinged, some modern designs will swivel on a pivot, others are designed to slide open.

Security is of course a prime factor. If the door fronts directly onto the street, you would be well advised to install a security gate of some kind. And of course a solid door would be a lot more appropriate than one with glass panes, but if your door is of the paned variety and you are reluctant to replace it, fit frosted or stained glass panels to obscure vision, the latter with protective shatterproof glass.

RIGHT   A *cat waits expectantly outside the entrance to a home with a simple portico and white-panelled front door.*

OPPOSITE
ABOVE LEFT   A *decorative hood over the entrance to a pretty, pink timber house is also practical in rainy weather.*

ABOVE RIGHT   *Iceberg roses complement the colour theme of this blue and white house, which features a contrasting wooden door.*

BELOW LEFT   *Yellow flowers in pots complement the painted front door.*

BELOW RIGHT   *Plants in two simple pots define the front entrance to a modern home.*

The architecture of the front entrance is also important. A porch or portico over the door will blend well with many house styles. Such a feature may be as elaborate or simple as you wish: it can introduce a feeling of understated grandeur, or otherwise give character to a dull entrance, or simply serve a practical function (providing shelter from the elements, for example, and protection for entrance lighting).

Period homes often feature elaborate canopies with classical columns or pilasters, while a more ordinary house will have a simple covering – either sloping or pitched, depending on the style of the roof.

The front door may be painted or, in the case of wood, stained or sealed. If paint is your choice, select a colour that matches the window frames and other woodwork and use this for the door frame with, perhaps, a contrasting hue for the door itself.

Plants, too, can add a decorative dimension to the entrance. Pots strategically placed on either side of the front door, or window boxes along the facade, will provide colour and character, fragrance and a welcome feel. Where there is a verandah, consider hanging baskets massed around the door or spaced along the front of the house.

An unusual colonnaded walkway designed by architect Peter Loebenberg.

OPPOSITE *A charming pathway vanishes beyond a mélange of shrubs and trees.*

WALKWAYS AND PATHS

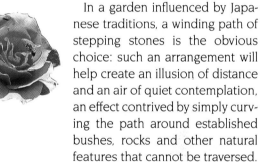

According to the dictionary definition, a path is simply a 'footway' or track along which people and things move and is not, usually, specially constructed. However, in the context of garden design, any sort of walkway is an important element of the overall scheme, both in terms of layout and the materials used.

The number of pathways incorporated into the garden design will depend on the size of the property and on the features, or areas, to which you want to create direct access. You will need a dry and solid surface to the house itself; a variety of other walkways may lead to garden seating, a swimming pool, summerhouse or perhaps simply to a beautiful view. You will also want to establish pathways through herb and vegetable gardens.

If the overall design is to be formal, in imitation perhaps of the classical European gardens of the past, plan a straight path from entrance to front door; if on the other hand your preference is for an English Country or cottagey look, a gently curving path would be more appropriate.

In a garden influenced by Japanese traditions, a winding path of stepping stones is the obvious choice: such an arrangement will help create an illusion of distance and an air of quiet contemplation, an effect contrived by simply curving the path around established bushes, rocks and other natural features that cannot be traversed.

By contrast, a formal rose walk may be incorporated within a Victorian-type garden. Here, a generously proportioned walkway, at least 6 m (20 ft) long and bounded by cultivated beds about 1,2 m (4 ft) wide, leads to a feature of some sort: a statue on a pedestal, perhaps; a fountain or a traditional sundial.

It may not be necessary to contain the course of a path, but an edging (the Victorians are noted for their edging tiles) or hedge on either side of a path will often enhance its appeal. A low, clipped lavender hedge alongside a narrow path, for instance, looks pretty and has a sweet fragrance, as does a pergola or hooped metal framework covered in roses, honeysuckle or wisteria.

PATHWAYS

The layout of pathways is an important element of design. Once established, they will provide safe, dry access to the house; dictate the routes through the garden and, if so planned, help divide the property up into segments, linking areas of interest and function. A path also plays a visual role, and will thus have its effect on the overall appearance of the garden. If it winds, you will not be able to see everything from any one point, and the property will, as a consequence, appear larger.

Numerous materials may be used for pathways, among them bricks, precast concrete paving slabs, simulated flagstones, cobblestones and timber. Gravel is an inexpensive option and one well suited to Japanese- and Oriental-style gardens. Both saw-dust and bark chippings are appropriate to vegetable gardens. Grass may also be planted to form a reasonably wide path between expansive beds, though remember that considerable care and attention will be needed to keep it looking neat.

And, of course, different materials may be combined: bricks laid around paving slabs, for example; railway sleepers with a ground cover or herbs (creeping marjoram, thyme, pennyroyal or chamomile) planted in between; sliced logs set in the earth (like stepping stones) and surrounded by pebbles.

The material used will often determine the width of a path (for instance logs or stepping stones will be narrow; railway sleepers much wider. Generally, though, a path should not be less than about 1 m (3 ft) wide to encourage a leisurely pace (width has a subconscious effect on the rate at which one moves: the narrower the path, or the steeper the steps, the faster one is encouraged to go).

If your preference is for stepping stones (popular in Japanese gardens) rather than a continuous pathway, ensure that they have reasonably flat tops – which does not mean, though, that they have to be absolutely level: indeed, irregular heights as well as shapes will add considerable interest. The type of material will tend to dictate the shape of stepping stones: cut stone and simulated flagstones will generally be square or rectangular, while precast slabs and cut logs (which are attractive, but tend to become slippery when wet) may be circular.

RIGHT *Precast concrete slabs wind enticingly through well-established ground covers and shrubbery.*

OPPOSITE
ABOVE LEFT *A stepping stone path allows easy access through an expansive bed to the house.*

ABOVE RIGHT *A stepping stone pathway leads to the pool area in a beautifully manicured garden.*

BELOW LEFT *A carefully contrived pathway of mixed materials adds interest to the garden.*

BELOW RIGHT *Ground covers have almost smothered a stone pathway in this charmingly overgrown garden.*

STEPS

The most common solution to a change in level is to construct steps of some kind – to entrances or doorways that are raised above the ground, for example; on steeply sloping sites, allowing access to areas that would otherwise be denied us; and in gardens that feature formal terraces and patios on higher or lower ground.

Steps also invite one to explore further and are thus appropriate at the entrance to an enclosed area within a garden (a patio, courtyard, old-fashioned rose garden, or simply a secluded retreat). This, though, presupposes the area's surface will either be slightly sunken or raised.

Outdoor steps may be constructed out of many different materials and in a wide variety of styles; among the options are circular designs built in brick; balustraded concrete structures leading from verandahs and formal raised patios; right-angled flights of stairs linking terraces; and beautifully simple log or stone steps. Generally though, steps designed for the garden are more modest, less formal than those that lead into the house.

Although interior stairways can be fairly steep (for safety reasons the dimensions of the tread must be at least 250 mm x 250 mm, with risers no more than 200 mm high), success in the garden usually depends on generosity of proportion and simplicity of style. Risers should preferably be slight and treads as broad as possible, enabling those who use them to do so in a relaxed, leisurely fashion. Their width should always be consistent with the path. Whereas interior stairways are essentially practical structures, exterior steps should also be reasonably decorative.

And they must of course be safe. If a potentially slippery material is used (railway sleepers, for example), it would be sensible to backfill with earth behind the timber treads and plant with a hardy ground cover or herbs to provide a grip.

RIGHT *Flowers edge brick steps, which link two different levels within a garden.*

OPPOSITE
ABOVE LEFT *Charming curved stone steps are softened by pink flowering plants.*

ABOVE RIGHT *An informal pebble-paved stairway, complete with cactii.*

BELOW LEFT *Giant logs define the approach to a farm swimming pool.*

BELOW RIGHT *Stone steps blend beautifully with an expansive natural rockery.*

DOORWAYS, GATES AND ARCHES

Unlike those incorporated in the boundary plan, garden doors and gates usually do not have a security function: they merely lead you from one section to another, and are often located in a hedge or trellis screen, seductively offering you a glimpse of what lies beyond. Unless their purpose is to provide total privacy or to give access to an ugly walled utility, they are seldom solid (comprising, at most, a wooden or iron see-through gate).

Indeed, a gateway may just be implied – by leaving an opening in a hedge or screen of informal plants, for instance. Alternatively an arch, planted with a scented creeper or climber, will add charm to a garden vista and create a pretty frame around that section of the garden which lies ahead; or it may even be located in a freestanding position, over a path bordered by shrubs and flowers.

Arches are commonly made from timber or metal which may or may not be curved. A wooden structure of gum poles may initially have a straight-lined top but, once planted, will assume an archlike form. An archway can even be created by training climbing plants up poles placed on either side of a path and encouraging them to intertwine over the top.

There are a great many plants that can be used to cover an arch, though those with fragrance are usually preferred: honeysuckle (Cape honeysuckle, *Tecomaria capensis* – indigenous to parts of southern Africa – will do well provided the region is not subject to severe frost), jasmine (both poet's jasmine, *Jasminum officinale* and Chinese jasmine, J. *polyanthum*, with its pretty flowers, have a deliciously fragrant scent) and wisteria (the deciduous W. *sinensis* is especially beautiful when covered in lavender-blue flowers). Rambling roses are another favourite, which are well suited to the Cottage or Victorian style.

RIGHT *An arched doorway leads from an attractively planted swimming pool area.*

OPPOSITE
ABOVE LEFT *Pink roses casacade over an arched entrance.*

ABOVE RIGHT *Stone steps pass under an arch linking two levels of an English Country garden.*

BELOW LEFT *A freestanding archway mirrors a niche.*

BELOW RIGHT *Roses are trained over arches, which define a strip driveway leading to an elegant country home.*

A graphic wooden structure defines the timber decked patio of an ultra-modern townhouse. Design: John Rushmere.

OPPOSITE Fibreglass sheeting provides shelter from all the elements and enables one to leave all types of furniture outdoors on this expansive brick paved patio.

PATIOS

More than any other outside areas, it is the patio, courtyard and terrace that will enable you to extend your house to create the indoor-outdoor lifestyle most of us have come to value so much.

According to the dictionary, a patio is an inner courtyard which is open to the sky, or a roofless paved area attached to the side of the house. Historically, the term was used specifically to describe the traditional inner courtyard of a Spanish house, but its modern usage encompasses a variety of decks and terraces, and virtually all open-air areas which extend our living space. Even a porch or verandah (both of which are usually roofed) will fall under the general definition.

The feature common to most of these outdoor areas is their hard, durable floor surface. The choice of material is wide; encompassing a range of raw materials that are freely available to you – local stone, pebbles, logs may be used; if your house is of facebrick, paving the patio or courtyard in a similar colour will visually link the two elements.

The general look of your outdoor area will also affect the choice of materials. A chequerboard of stone and moss makes an attractive patio floor in a Japanese-style garden, while a marble terrace is more appropriate to one designed on European lines. Brick, one of the most practical of choices, is well suited to many different garden types.

The decorative features of your patio, too, will be influenced by both interior and exterior finishes. Tubs and pots grouped together can be most effective; ceramic pots fashioned in the Oriental style will complement a minimalistic Japanese or perhaps a Chinese decorative approach, while more rustic terracotta containers will be more appropriate if your home has a Mediterranean, Cottage or even a Farmhouse look. Or you may prefer to simply brighten the area with painted pots.

Planting should also be complementary: choose something like an ornamental bamboo (Nandina domestica, also known as sacred bamboo, is a possibility) for the Oriental pots; plant the more earthy containers with herbs or colourful annuals.

THE TERRACE

An effect similar to terracing was achieved by the builders of the ancient Hanging Gardens of Babylon, where a series of long plots were vaulted so that they could be watered directly from the Euphrates River. However, the garden terrace as we know it probably had humbler origins – in subsistence farming, where the land sloped and could only be cultivated properly if levelled in some way to prevent erosion of the topsoil.

The basic technique these farmers developed was to remove the fertile ground and shift the subsoil to form wide, level areas. They then built a wall of some sort (often simply of dry stone) to retain the earth before replacing the topsoil for planting.

On some steep plots, it is possible to dig or cut into the bank, filling the lower section with compacted earth to create what is, in effect, a level terrace for building. In these instances (particularly if the gradient is 30 degrees or more), the garden will also have to be terraced if it is to be functional.

One of the prime ingredients of a successful terrace is the low retaining wall that holds it in place. This may, as we have seen, be built from random stone, in the form of a dry wall or with bricks or cut stone and mortar. Railway sleepers are also an option. Whichever material is chosen, make sure that there is adequate drainage.

RIGHT   *Split poles have been used effectively to terrace a steeply sloping site.*

OPPOSITE
ABOVE LEFT   *Brick and stone form terraces.*

ABOVE RIGHT   *A balustraded brick paved terrace.*

BELOW LEFT   *Terraced flowerbeds planted with annuals.*

BELOW RIGHT   *Grassed terraces retained by brick walls.*

Terraces, especially those close to the house, are often given a hard surface finish. And of course they may be lawned, perhaps with a pathway running alongside flower beds. Other materials are much the same as those recommended for patio areas and include brick, reconstituted stone and 'crazy paving'. Marble is a logical (though relatively expensive) choice for the terrace floor in a garden created in the traditional European styles.

The height of each terrace will, obviously, depend on the nature of the site. The higher structures may have to be edged with a railing of some kind, and here precast concrete balustrades (made in designs similar to the traditional stone varieties), and wrought-ironwork are two possibilities. Simpler options are the post-and-rail fence, or a rudimentary barrier created with upright pieces of timber with thick rope strung between them.

The area below a terrace is ideal for a parterre (see pages 17, 18, 30 and page 204) and which will give it a distinctly European flavour.

A paved space adjacent to the house, but raised and fairly long and narrow, is often called a terrace rather than a patio. Often formal in style, these areas tend to be symmetrical in design, with urns and statues creating the appropriately classical effect.

THE TIMBER DECK

Wooden decking is a popular choice for sloping properties, principally because it enables one to reclaim land that would otherwise be unusable. Decking, however, is not limited to this type of site: supported on sturdy posts and beams, it may be raised just a few centimetres above the ground to level an irregular area or one that becomes water-logged during the wet, rainy season, or perhaps to accommodate a hot water spa (see page 195).

A timber deck is often constructed as an alternative to the orthodox verandah, creating a low-maintenance area which can be used for outdoor living and entertaining. Or it may be erected around a swimming pool, a water garden or pond.

If the plot does slope, a series of decks may be built to create terraces – a particularly impressive arrangement if each platform is placed at a different angle. Alternatively, the timber terracing may be used in conjunction with other materials, leading perhaps to a brick paved or tiled patio. In most instances, a wooden pergola built overhead will further enhance the effect.

One major advantage of timber decking is that it conforms with most house styles – both new and old. However, it will suit some outdoor areas better than others: it is particularly appropriate to Japanese-style and natural-look gardens.

Decking wood is usually treated (to avoid infestation and rot) or varnished, but a really good-quality hardwood, such as teak, may simply be left to weather to a dull, earthy grey.

Certain types of timber are better suited to different areas. Although the choice will be limited by availability and by price, some of the most popular varieties are afrormosia, an attractive yellow-brown West African hardwood; balau, a fine textured wood noted for its strength and durability in hot, humid climates; beech, which is straight-grained and pale in colour; Californian redwood, imported from that region and valued for its resistance to decay and infestation; cerejeira, a pinkish wood that is easy to work with; oak (in particular American red and American white), which is attractive, strong and versatile; Philippine mahogany, a durable timber that varies in colour from light to dark red; teak, undoubtedly the best quality timber available; and meranti, a versatile Malaysian wood.

OPPOSITE   A *suspended wooden deck is the perfect place for outdoor living. Design: Clara da Cruz Almeida.*

RIGHT   A *hot water spa set in an attractive deck with a magnificent sea view.*

PAVED PATIOS

Where doors open out onto the garden, it is usually advisable – for practical reasons – to create a patio of some sort in order to make good use of the area immediately outside the house (and to prevent people from tramping mud and dirt inside). In this instance, paving may be of brick or any other hard material that blends with the indoor finishes. Tiles, for instance, carried through for continuity (provided they have a matt finish), or stone, marble or even timber, may be used successfully.

On the other hand a patio may be a freestanding area within the garden itself – around and adjacent to a swimming pool or spa, for example. Here one could screen the area with trellis or an open block wall, or perhaps plant an informal hedge for protection against the prevailing wind. Such screening will generally heighten the impression of an outdoor 'living room', and indeed will enhance the garden scheme as a whole.

Wherever it is sited, the floor of the patio should be hard-wearing and practical. Brick is a common option, although other materials are also suitable, the choice depending largely on the function the area will fulfil. If you intend using the patio for alfresco eating, for example, a major factor will be the evenness of the surface – it should be level enough to accommodate a table that will not wobble. If it is located next to the pool area, ensure that the surface will not become slippery (and therefore dangerous) when wet.

Additional features here – a barbecue, built-in seating and permanent eating areas – are commonly incorporated to make maximum use of the patio area.

The patio will often benefit from some form of screening and shelter. Walling (see pages 85-88) and enclosures can be of brick, fencing, planted screens or trelliswork, while overhead protection may be provided by a canvas or aluminium awning over a pergola; by a quick-growing climber or vine; or by covering the structure with shadecloth or a more permanent roofing such as fibreglass.

RIGHT *Double doors open onto an informal paved patio.*

OPPOSITE
ABOVE LEFT *A sheltered patio is perfect for entertaining.*

ABOVE RIGHT *A tiled patio overlooking the sea has open sides, but is sheltered overhead by a retractable canvas awning.*

BELOW LEFT *A vine-covered pergola adds to the charm of a patio used for alfresco meals.*

BELOW RIGHT *A canvas awning shelters a paved patio.*

THE COURTYARD

The origins of the modern courtyard may be traced to the atria of classical Roman villas and the internal patios of medieval Spain. This area – which was also the prototype of today's patio – served as the outdoor 'living room' and was entirely encircled by the house, with doors from all accessible rooms leading onto it. There were few, if any, windows on the outside walls, so the area became a sheltered and totally private retreat. It was open to the sky, and invariably decorated with statues, a variety of planted containers, an ornamental pool and perhaps a fountain. All in all, the courtyard of old seems a very romantic place to us, evoking images of balmy Mediterranean summers, glowing sunsets and translucent azure-hued seas.

The modern courtyard can also be a wonderfully intimate and secluded area.

It is usually bounded by the house on three sides, sometimes on all four, and there is no immediate access from the street, so providing the kind of privacy and intimacy that is impossible to contrive elsewhere in the garden.

However, courtyards can have their drawbacks: they are frequently either suntraps or, conversely, gloomy places that do not attract much sunlight at all. Painting the walls white – or a light colour – will often help, as will clever planting to create a lushly tropical effect.

Water is also an important element – a small pond, for example, or even a simple wall-mounted fountain that trickles into a bowl or shell, will introduce both freshness and tranquillity.

Most courtyards have hard, durable surfaces. Suitable materials include brick paving, quarry tiles, stone and, if you like and can afford it, marble.

The size of the courtyard will determine the planting pattern, but it is here, perhaps more than anywhere else, that the vertical approach will succeed. Train climbers and creepers up walls and freestanding supports. These and other plants may be established in containers (see page 112) or, if the area does not have a hard surface, set directly in the ground.

OPPOSITE   *An unusual Mediterranean-style courtyard designed by Clara da Cruz Almeida and colour co-ordinated by Heber van Zyl.*

RIGHT   *A shady courtyard with an abundance of plants is an inviting place for alfresco entertaining.*

ROOF GARDENS AND VERANDAHS

Balconies, verandahs and, in the case of a flat-roofed building, roof gardens are generally designed as an integral part of the house itself. Although different in character, each of them extends the useable area of the house, allowing for an indoor-outdoor lifestyle. They also provide the opportunity for effective container gardening.

When it comes to style, the verandah in particular presents enormously varied possibilities, ranging from the plainest of wooden designs to one that incorporates the elaborate cast-ironwork so popular during the Victorian period. Much will depend on the style of the house itself and on the location of the property. Traditional colonial-type verandahs, for example, are still common in parts of Australia, America and South Africa – all countries in which sultry weather conditions are often experienced.

The size, and therefore the usefulness, of the structure will be governed by architectural factors. A small balcony will enable you to open the doors of an upper-storey room to allow extra light and fresh air to enter; a generous verandah will provide the opportunity for alfresco eating and, if it is sheltered, for entertaining in all weather conditions.

RIGHT   A *covered Victorian-style verandah.*

OPPOSITE
ABOVE LEFT   *The verandah of Zorgvliet, an 18th century Cape Dutch house in Cape Town, South Africa, was Victorianized in about 1860.*

ABOVE RIGHT   *Bougainvillaea spills onto a verandah.*

BELOW LEFT   *Traditional pillars line the verandah at Groote Schuur, once the Cape Town home of South African mining magnate Cecil John Rhodes.*

BELOW RIGHT   *An attractive seating area on a patio.*

While the orthodox patio, often serving as a kind of flexible extension to the house, is always at ground level, the roof garden is more usually a feature of the top-storey, or penthouse, apartment. Many flat-dwellers do not enjoy access to ground-level gardens but, with suitable roof space, they too can have an outdoor area. The structure will of course have to be strong enough to take the weight of soil, plants, containers and, in some instances, the water needed to fill a pool. But then the garden does not have to be a grand affair: even the most meagre roof terrace can usually be enhanced by a selection of plants displayed in pots and tubs.

Since roof gardens are generally open to the sky (and therefore totally exposed to the elements), a pergola or awning will need to be erected if it is to be in use all year round, or if furniture is to be left exposed. For practical reasons, lighter structures (timber or aluminium) are the most suitable.

A pergola may be covered with canvas, shadecloth or with a creeper or vine grown in a large pot; or shade can be provided by umbrellas (co-ordinating colours with those of the flowering plants).

Trelliswork or bamboo screens will also help reduce the effect of wind. Solid barriers, on the other hand, are not a good idea: they block the wind, but create turbulence as it bounces off the structure.

Before creating a roof garden, check the structural capabilities of the area (with an engineer if necessary), and ensure that it is totally waterproof: plants will require regular watering, which will expose the roof to more moisture than rain normally brings.

The metal structure of a traditional-style pavilion frames the house at the top of a long, stepped walkway.

OPPOSITE

ABOVE LEFT   *A Lutyens-style timber bridge is tucked away at the bottom of an impressive and unusual garden designed by Patrick Watson.*

ABOVE RIGHT   *Logs have been used to create an attractive bridge feature softened by green foliage.*

BELOW LEFT   *An architectural structure designed to add character to a patio.*

BELOW RIGHT   *Swimming pool change-rooms created during the 1960s, in the Victorian style.*

STRUCTURES

Most properties incorporate some kind of structure, whether it be simply a boundary wall or fence (see pages 85-88) designed for privacy, or a screen of some sort to partition the garden or prevent unnecessary noise; steps to cope with gradients; doorways and arches built of bricks and mortar, stone, or wrought iron. Even more a part of the modern garden are practical structures: carports, barbecues and built-in furniture (discussed in a separate section on Seating, see pages 159-165) and so on.

Treillage is not too often found these days, but is certainly something to be considered. Common in 18th-century France, this is an art that involves fairly flimsy trelliswork in the construction of what appears to be an elaborate architectural feature, so adding a dimension of *trompe l'oeil* (designed to 'deceive the eye') to the garden. Less ornate and complex versions may be created to screen, or simply to add height to a wall or to support climbers. If designed in the traditional manner, these can also lend perspective to even the tiniest garden.

As always, the type and style of the garden will dictate those structures that will both be practical and enhance its visual character. If, for instance, you have your heart set on a pretty, arched bridge but do not have a stream or sizeable ditch of some kind, you will either have to create a water garden or pond, or abandon the idea altogether. And then there are the stylistic dictates: if yours is a contemplative Japanese garden, a large barbecue structure with chimney and pizza oven would simply look absurd. Conversely, a fussy Victorian garden will not be convincing without a gazebo or pavilion, and a rambling English Country garden should have at least one pergola, as should any Mediterranean-style exterior.

Of course not all gardens, or indeed houses, are built according to a particular style, and here it is the materials and proportions that assume importance. For instance, whilst gum poles are acceptable in most garden settings, an authentic Lutyens (see page 43) pergola will combine brick or stone uprights with planed timber cross-pieces.

THE ARBOUR AND PERGOLA

Perhaps the simplest of garden structures, pergolas and arbours commonly serve as forms of shelter (see pages 97-102), and also as effective screening devices, often introduced to divide the garden into sections, or to hide certain features (such as the washing line or compost heap) from view. Since they can be freestanding units, they will introduce height variation to an uninteresting outdoor area. They may also be used for roof gardens. And they make wonderful supports for climbers and ramblers: once the plants are established, they become beautifully decorative features in themselves.

Found in gardens of all shapes and sizes, a pergola is often built as a walkway, covered with vines or some other climbing or trailing plant, attracting and focusing the vision. It may also be constructed over a driveway, giving dappled shade overhead, or over a carport in place of a solid roof, or attached to the house to provide shelter for informal entertaining.

Popular in parts of America, South Africa and other countries with similarly moderate climates, pergolas may be built of wood or a combination of timber beams and cross-pieces and stone or brick piers.

Often incorporated in designs by the renowned Edwin Lutyens and Gertrude Jekyll (see pages 38, 41, 42, 43 and 99), this type of structure is now found all over the world in many different styles of garden.

A traditional arbour – which, unlike an ordinary pergola, does not lead anywhere or even cover any substantial area – is a standard feature of the Victorian-style garden (even though its origins seem to lie in Continental Europe rather than England). There is a hint of the romantic about such a feature, so it would be an appropriate addition to the secluded or secret garden.

The arbour is particularly well suited to the small property, since it may be established on the perimeter, thus creating the impression that the garden extends beyond the boundary.

By tradition simple in structure, arbours are quickly erected, using timber uprights and flexible branches or wire to form an arch over a bench or even a turf seat (see page 161) or earth bank planted with chamomile. Choose a quick-growing climber like scented honeysuckle, or one of the clematis species, and you will be sure to have an established feature within a season or two.

RIGHT   A *simple pergola supports climbing plants.*

OPPOSITE
ABOVE LEFT   *Bamboo has been used to create an attractive arbour. Design: Gary Bartsh.*

ABOVE RIGHT   *A leafy arbour in a garden originally laid out by Sir Herbert Baker.*

BELOW LEFT   *A simple wooden, booth-like arbour shelters a flourishing pot plant.*

BELOW RIGHT   *A freestanding pergola constructed alongside a swimming pool.*

THE SUMMERHOUSE AND GAZEBO

While contemporary gazebos and summerhouses are not generally as detailed and ornamental as those constructed in either classical or period gardens, they will usually fulfil both decorative and practical functions, giving shelter (see pages 97-102) and forming an attractive focal point. A well designed summerhouse may, in the absence of a garden shed (see page 171), even be used for storing moveable garden furniture and cushions, tools and swimming pool equipment.

When planning a summerhouse or gazebo, therefore, carefully consider its intended uses. If you want refuge, a place to spend time quietly reading and relaxing, away from the distraction of children and the hustle and bustle of the household, you would not site it within earshot of the swimming pool. If, however, the structure is to be used for entertainment, alfresco meals and so on, then the pool would be a sensible location.

Style, though, is linked as much to the general garden scheme as to function. A small open-sided summerhouse or gazebo, for example, will not be much use if you need it to store garden tools, furniture and so on. Similarly, a timber cabin would not serve both as a greenhouse for plant propagation and as a summerhouse.

If you have a liking for the eclectic eccentricities popularized by the Victorians, consider an elaborate gazebo: a small pagoda or Chinese pavilion would suit an Oriental-style garden; a more classical summerhouse will be a better choice for a formal garden that imitates the early European style. Whatever you decide to build must also fit into the overall garden scheme and complement the other features.

If you are planning (or already have) a permanent outdoor cooking area and want some additional form of shelter from the sun or wind, make sure the two structures are harmonious in their design. A no-nonsense brick barbecue will look out of place alongside a pretty hexagonal timber gazebo, just as a plastered and chimneyed Mediterranean-style barbecue would be absurd near a thatch-roofed stone summerhouse.

RIGHT A *pretty Victorian-style gazebo, complete with carpenter's lace and blue-painted weathercock and vane.*

OPPOSITE
ABOVE LEFT A *thatch-roofed shelter, partly enclosed to form a garden pub.*

ABOVE RIGHT An *attractive pavilion set alongside a tennis court is an ideal venue for spectators.*

BELOW LEFT A *charming Victorian-style gazebo fulfils both decorative and practical functions.*

BELOW RIGHT *This traditional summerhouse is spacious enough to accommodate overnight guests.*

THE BARBECUE

A built-in barbecue is a popular permanent structure in most countries and areas which enjoy moderate climatic conditions.

The type of structure, and the area of the garden in which it is to be sited, will of course depend on the family's needs and lifestyle. Perhaps the two most common locations are, first, beside a swimming pool (see pages 191-192) and, second, on a patio that is near (or attached to) the house. In the smaller garden, it may be incorporated into a boundary wall or on a more elaborate patio, combined with seating, planters and so on.

Ideally a barbecue should be sited near enough to the kitchen so that the conveyance of food, plates and other items which cannot be stored nearby does not become a problem. And it is important to position the barbecue so that the prevailing wind will blow smoke away from the area. Alternatively incorporate a chimney in the design.

If you plan to use this outdoor cooking facility frequently, not only should the design be able to cope with the numbers you will be providing for, but have adequate storage for all the usual utensils (cooking forks, tongs, spatulas and so on), wood and charcoal. You may also want to accommodate a traditional cast-iron pot alongside the conventional grill, and perhaps even a pizza oven or one that may be used for baking bread.

One of the most basic barbecue designs comprises a slightly sunken fire pit which may be used with a grid, or to accommodate a cast-iron pot suspended over the fire on a steel pole of some sort.

More popular, though, are structures that allow one to cook without crouching, and which have storage beneath the fire surface, for a range of items not ordinarily required in the kitchen.

The most common material used for building a structure of this sort is clay brick, although stone is another suitable option. If concrete bricks are your choice, use fire bricks for the surface on which the fire will be made to prevent the concrete from cracking. Do not use a concrete paving slab for the fire bed as it will not withstand the heat and will inevitably crack, and if you incorporate concrete lintels, lay fire bricks or pavers over them.

RIGHT *An attractive barbecue with built-in seating and a tiled working surface is located alongside a thatched summerhouse.*

OPPOSITE
ABOVE LEFT *A neat, compact and good-looking barbecue design is sheltered with yellow shadecloth.*

ABOVE RIGHT *Shadecloth provides partial shelter over a charming outdoor cooking and entertainment area.*

BELOW LEFT *Natural materials — timber, quarry tiles and brick paving — contribute to the appeal of a simple barbecue design in a small garden.*

BELOW RIGHT *Instead of supporting the pergola with an ordinary pillar, a simple barbecue has been incorporated.*

THE CARPORT

A carport is a permanent structure frequently included in the outdoor plan of contemporary homes – sometimes even where there is a garage (it is often erected to give some shelter to a second vehicle, or it may be that the garage is being used for another purpose; as a storeroom or workshop, or has been converted for additional living space).

Reasonably inexpensive to construct, most carports resemble pergolas (see page 151) and are built from similar materials. Uprights may be of poles or cut timber, galvanized steel, brick, stone or even precast pillars, while cross-pieces are usually of wood (gum poles or planed timber). If the carport is to protect vehicles from the elements, a solid covering (fibreglass, aluminium, corrugated iron, fibrecement and polycarbonate sheeting are all possible options) will have to be incorporated. Reasonably waterproof bituminous felt, shadecloth (which is available in a wide range of colours both pastel and primary) and dense creepers will all provide a shield from the sun's harmful rays.

When planning a carport, consider designs and materials that fit in with the style of your house and any other buildings on the property. Facebrick pillars combined with a fibreglass roof will protect your car and, well built, can look attractive, but they will not enhance a pretty Victorian cottage. Similarly, a rustic gum pole structure should be avoided if yours is a chic, modern house.

Carports are often built alongside garages and boundary walls, so the materials used for the parking surface should ideally be the same as those used for the driveway (see page 125). Brick paving, interlocking concrete road stones and asphalt are all common, and suitable, options. Gravel, concrete, slate and pebble paving are other possibilities.

RIGHT   *Precast pillars support timber cross-pieces smothered by colourful bougainvillaea.*

OPPOSITE
ABOVE LEFT   *A double carport with protective fibreglass roof is attractive and practical.*

ABOVE RIGHT   *A carport with trellised sides and a solid roof structure.*

BELOW LEFT   *The sturdy capped pillars of a double carport adds style to the structure.*

BELOW RIGHT   *An attractive lean-to type carport provides added protection alongside a double garage.*

A *green metal bench provides a restful seating place in an attractive secret garden which has been designed in the English Country style.*

OPPOSITE *Cushion-covered loungers and chairs provide versatile seating on a barbecue patio located next to a tropical swimming pool.*

SEATING

In a home where the emphasis is on an indoor-outdoor flow – where the living area extends to the outside – the convenience and practicality of garden furniture is a prime consideration. The positioning of benches, chairs, tables and so forth is important; seat designs should be well chosen for truly inviting relaxation. Any form of seating should invite you to stop and rest for a while. If there is a view to be enjoyed, benches should be sited for the best outlook possible.

Sun and shade are vital elements, and are directly linked to function. A seat and table for alfresco eating, for example, should be sited under shelter, perhaps beneath a leafy arbour or vine-covered pergola – where there will be at least some protection from both the direct rays of the sun and the prevailing wind. If you plan to use it frequently, throughout the seasons, a more permanent form of covering may, however, be necessary (see pages 97-102). Poolside seating should be so positioned that those using it are exposed (at least for part of the day) to the sun. Seating alongside a tennis court, on the other hand, should be sheltered for all those watching the game.

Of course, much depends on whether you want a permanent arrangement, or one that can easily be altered. Some kinds of chair and bench – those made from wrought iron, or a hardwood like teak for instance – may be left outdoors without any fear of deterioration, while others must be taken inside when not in use. Or you may prefer to build seating from bricks and mortar, or perhaps natural stone, incorporating it into a patio wall or combining it with your braai design (see page 155) along with a suitable working surface and storage.

There are many types of seating suitable for outdoor living, some best suited to patios, others to the garden itself, all of which are available in a wide selection of styles. Nevertheless, wherever it is to be located, and whatever its type and style, an outdoor seat should be both decorative and functional.

This need not be a disadvantage as most types of movable furniture may be used in a variety of locations at different times.

NATURAL SEATING

It is not always necessary to use man-made designs for garden seating: natural rock formations, cut logs and even earth banks will all provide a place to sit. These may not initially be an easily used form, but with thoughtful placing and perhaps a little minor conversion it is often possible to create something quite special and attractive.

A particularly unusual option is the turf bench, modelled on those seen in paintings of medieval gardens. The simplest method of construction here is to build the sides from brick or railway sleepers, and then to plant grass, or herbs, of the kind that will trail over the edges to cover and soften the hard material. But a word of warning: although the idea is to sit on a mattress of sweet-smelling herbs (thyme, chamomile and pennyroyal are all good choices), most plants will tend to remain damp, even in dry weather, so it would be prudent to lay a few paving slabs or large, flat stones across the top surface of this kind of structure.

Another quick and reasonably easy way of adapting natural features is to slice the trunk of an unwanted tree to form chairs and perhaps even a small table. This may not prove the most comfortable of seating arrangements, but it is a good option in the wild garden or meadow, and one which is especially popular, practical (and furthermore inexpensive) for a children's play area.

If yours is to be a Cottage-style garden, follow the example of the old cottagers by digging two stout logs into the ground and securing a plank across the top. Alternatively, if stone is plentiful in your area, you may prefer to use this for the supports, perhaps with a rustic timber seating surface. Where there is a natural stream or rocky outcrop, suitable stones may serve as *in situ* seating.

RIGHT *Cut logs make an effective support for rustic seating. The base of a tree trunk has been left in place, forming a flat surface that can be used as a table.*

OPPOSITE *A natural looking beach pool is a good location for a bench made from two wooden stumps and a railway sleeper. A dead tree trunk is also utilized as a seat.*

PERMANENT DESIGNS

The range of manufactured seating intended for permanent outdoor use is not limited to materials that will withstand weathering. Climate, therefore is a vital consideration. For instance, if you live in a high rainfall area, ensure that your choice will not deteriorate in the wet season.

Even though it is not commonly used for contemporary outdoor furniture, stone is one of the most handsome of natural materials available. Permanent designs may be built in brick, with either a brick, concrete or wooden seating surface, and – for a touch of individuality – can be banked up with earth, fronted with brick or even wood, and planted with chamomile or herbs (see page 161).

Marble, too, will produce beautiful results, though it is fairly expensive. It is sometimes laid in tile or mosaic form over built-in seating around spa or pool areas or even on terraces.

Concrete is a versatile material: not only will it withstand all weather conditions, but it improves its appearance as moss and algae begin to form. Various designs are available, including solid slabs set on a selection of pedestals and balusters (both simple and elaborate), and a range of benches that usually come with matching tables. Some of these are made in imitation of early stone and marble seats and have attractively ornamental backs.

RIGHT   *Timber seating designed to be left outdoors.*

OPPOSITE
ABOVE LEFT   *Built-in seating is enhanced by the addition of comfortable cushions.*

ABOVE RIGHT   *A seat with a colourful mosaic top.*

BELOW LEFT   *A polished granite table and benches.*

BELOW RIGHT   *Tiles are a practical finish for seating.*

Cast-iron furniture is popular and elegant, and will withstand the elements. Many of the units on the market are patterned on early designs and will therefore suit the more traditional type of garden.

Some wooden benches may be permanent garden features, since they are robust enough to be left outside in all weather conditions. These are, however, usually of the simpler designs (the more ornate, carved types are usually reserved for use under cover). Hardwoods are preferred: teak, for instance, is slow to season and will weather well, while some of the softwoods will tend to warp and rot in a fairly short period of time.

Maintenance of outdoor wooden furniture will be more demanding than for other materials as it will have to be regularly treated – or painted. While moss and lichen looks wonderful on stone or concrete, it should not be allowed to get a hold on timber.

Timber may also be used to make built-in seats in the garden. Among the most successful designs are those intended for patios and barbecue areas, and those installed around the trunk of sturdy trees.

Whatever the material used, permanent seating usually benefits from the addition of colourful, comfortable cushions. These accessories will, of course, have to be stored away when not in use.

MOVABLE FURNITURE

There are a number of functional portable garden furniture designs on the market, the most common of them made of hardy, weather-proof plastic. Available are chairs, loungers, tables and even portable drinks trolleys; the stackable chairs are particularly useful for properties where space is at a premium.

Also common are the folding canvas deck chairs, popular director's chairs (with a wooden or metal framework), and attractive folding wooden seats manufactured to designs used on ocean liners and in European parks. These have an elegance that much of the ordinary folding furniture on the market lacks. All may be used with a variety of tables, including those which also fold.

Cane and wicker furniture looks attractive on verandahs and covered patios. If yours is a Victorian-style house, Lloyd loom chairs (which are still made in Britain today), though expensive, are a good choice. Contemporary designs, however, are attractive enough, and will look just as effective on the verandah of a farmhouse or the porch of a country cottage. These materials should not be left in either the sun or rain as they will deteriorate fairly rapidly.

Although most metal furniture is left permanently in place, aluminium designs are lighter, more easily moveable and their position may therefore be changed as needed – beneath a sheltered pergola, perhaps, and carried out to a nearby terrace for alfresco meals when required.

Charming and easily portable additions to the garden are hammocks, which can be left out some of the time, but should be taken indoors in bad weather; and garden swing-seats (which were particularly popular in the 1960s and 1970s, though they are not much seen nowadays). Swing-seats are usually distinguished by colourful canvas cushions and awnings but are, unhappily, too often left out in the open to discolour and deteriorate.

RIGHT *Cane furniture is an appropriate choice on a covered patio sheltered from the elements.*

OPPOSITE
ABOVE LEFT *Movable furniture will deteriorate if left in the garden for any length of time.*

ABOVE RIGHT *Painted bentwood chairs encircle a wrought-iron table on a pretty Victorian-style verandah.*

BELOW LEFT *Cane bar stools and basket-weave furniture enliven a partially protected barbecue patio.*

BELOW RIGHT *Painted wooden chairs are used around a table left permanently in place.*

An unusual outbuilding, constructed in the style of a typical Japanese tea house, is set in a small Western garden designed in the genre by potter Steve Shapiro, who now uses it as a showroom for his work.

OPPOSITE Potted roses and colourful flowers brighten a simple thatched outbuilding that could easily be converted to form a useful summerhouse.

OUTBUILDINGS

Most of us devote a lot of time and effort to ensuring that our houses and gardens are neat, attractive and stylistically coherent, but when it comes down to outbuildings, one all to often finds a conglomeration of structures that are practical enough but visually unappealing. They also tend to be the last in line in terms of regular maintenance. And understandably so, perhaps: a leaking tool shed roof will rank lower on the list of priorities than a blocked and broken gutter which seeps onto the verandah; a smashed window in the living room will take precedence over broken panes in the greenhouse.

The range of outbuildings to be found on plots varies, depending on the area, and on the size and age of the property. In a new suburb proclaimed on what had been farmland, for instance, there might be a residue of sheds, chicken runs, pigsties, stables, even old long-drop toilets. In most old-established residential areas, the outbuildings are likely to have been designed as wood or tool sheds, domestic workers' quarters and so forth.

If you live in an older house, you may have inherited outbuildings that you do not want. Rather than demolish these, consider ways in which you can put them to new use. A shed, for instance, could be used as an outdoor playroom for children; a barn (not an uncommon structure if you live on a larger property in the country) as a studio or converted into a guest cottage. Neglected domestic workers' quarters dating from the earlier part of this century will often make a useful storeroom, or a changeroom for the swimming pool, or it may even be possible to convert them into a summerhouse.

However, if you do intend to demolish them – to make way for flowerbeds, for example – you will also have to remove foundations and any hardcore that may have been incorporated beneath them. In the case of planting, of course, topsoil, manure and so on will need to be dug in.

Any new outbuildings you are planning can usually be built on or near the boundaries of the property, so saving space.

THE GREENHOUSE

Relatively few people today bother themselves with greenhouses (which originated during the 17th century, when they were built to house evergreens). Yet these structures can be invaluable, especially in areas which experience regular winter frost.

Unlike the conservatory, which frequently doubles as a living area, the true greenhouse is a glassed hothouse designed to trap the sunlight and so protect the plants inside.

Even though a conservatory-type extension, including one that incorporates curved glass or a polycarbonate material, may easily double as a functional greenhouse, it is preferable to use a separate building for the purpose. Plants are not kept in a greenhouse for their decorative value, and you will need to water regularly (an automatic system can be most useful), repot, feed and so on, all of which can be extremely messy work.

A basic outhouse of this type is easily constructed around a framework of wood (of the type built by the English cottagers) or of metal – combined with glass, polycarbonate or fibreglass. Ideally the glass should extend to ground level, at least on one side, so allowing the maximum amount of sunlight to enter. Since glass will trap the sun's heat, it may also be necessary to have adjustable blinds to prevent excess light, or ventilators of some kind.

RIGHT   A *well-organized greenhouse.*

OPPOSITE
ABOVE LEFT   *Pots arranged on empty seed trays in a greenhouse covered by fibreglass sheeting.*

ABOVE RIGHT   A *greenhouse doubles as a garden shed.*

BELOW LEFT   A *Victorian-style greenhouse with glass roof.*

BELOW RIGHT   *Pelargoniums in a greenhouse.*

In days gone by, greenhouses were artificially heated to maintain a tropical environment. Nowadays, though, people seldom need to heat this artificial microclimate above subtropical temperatures (35 °C, or 13 °F, and higher).

The true greenhouse, with its controlled temperature, is highly labour-intensive, and certain exotic species will require a tropical hothouse. Unfortunately the cost factor is often inhibitive, so the option – especially in the northern hemisphere – is to lower one's sights, choosing the less demanding kinds of plant, ensuring merely that they are protected, under cover, from the more adverse elements (in particular hail, frost and high wind). Where harsh sunlight is a negative factor, a shade structure of some kind will often suffice.

All kinds of plants can be cultivated in a greenhouse. Some of the more popular varieties traditionally grown in this environment are chrysanthemums, fuchsias and pelargoniums (which are indigenous to South Africa, and therefore flourish in exposed positions in warmer climates). A greenhouse will also prove a sound investment if you are going to grow your annuals from seed, or if you plan to produce certain food crops – tomatoes and cucumbers, for example – throughout the year.

THE GARDEN SHED

Probably the most common outbuilding, the garden shed is an indispensable repository for tools – spades, forks, wheelbarrow, rake, watering cans, hose and the rest. It is also useful for storing bags of compost and fertilizer, pesticides (although these should be properly labelled and securely locked away in the interests of safety), and such swimming pool equipment as chlorine, acid and test kits.

If the shed is large enough, it may double as a workshop, although here you will have to install a power point. Good lighting (both natural and artificial) will be another essential, especially if you are going to use it for woodwork, metalwork, welding and so on, rather than simply for storing tools, sandpaper, hammers, and all the other items in the handyman's inventory.

Whatever its uses, though, you would most probably want to erect shelving and to include a work bench or table of some sort. Racks for storing root vegetables and fruit, and perhaps bulbs as well, are another useful addition. And there should of course be plenty of hooks for hanging tools neatly.

RIGHT   A *typical timber shed provides storage space for a lawn mower and other power tools.*

OPPOSITE
ABOVE LEFT   *An attractive split-pole shed in a backyard with a view.*

ABOVE RIGHT   *An old train carriage is now a garden shed with plenty of space for storage.*

BELOW LEFT   *A shed built from wood and fibreglass has a fibrecement roof.*

BELOW RIGHT   *A deteriorating summerhouse is now used as a garden shed.*

The most common material used in the construction of garden sheds is timber. Wooden sheds, in fact, are widely available in a prefabricated form, usually with bituminous felt-covered roofs. Most of these structures are unobtrusive enough in design, but should nevertheless be so positioned that they will not detract from the look of the house itself. If the shed is to be sited next to the house, it should, ideally, be built of materials that will complement the main dwelling.

A lean-to, either walled or open-sided, is another type of shed, usually constructed alongside a garage or other outbuilding wall, sometimes even abutting a boundary wall. Any type of roof sheeting may be used, but fibreglass is a popular option. Although useful for storing most gardening equipment, it is not generally practical for power tools, lawn mowers and so forth unless it has some kind of walling or screen (see pages 85-88) to protect expensive equipment from the elements.

HOME FOR AN ANIMAL

The most common suburban domestic animals are cats and dogs and, to lesser extent, rabbits, but there are still areas not very far from the major cities where horses, ducks, chickens, geese, cows and other farm animals may be kept.

While cats seldom require special accommodation – they make themselves at home inside the house – many family dogs are not allowed to sleep indoors. Wooden dog kennels (usually made of the same materials as those of prefabricated sheds) are widely available. Some people, though, prefer to make their own. Cottage gardens often included a dog kennel outside the back door of the house. It might have been a simple, wooden structure, similar to those mass-produced today, or a more elaborate creation made by the animal's owner, occasionally incorporating carpenter's lace.

Large wine-barrels may be cut in half to serve as an unusual kennel, or you could design a structure that complements the architecture of the house.

If you keep chickens, they may range freely during the day if you wish, but should preferably be kept in an enclosed pen of some kind at night. Traditionally, broody hens are confined in a coop, while the rooster has the run of the back yard. If you have an orchard, consider incorporating the run into this out-of-the-way area.

Ducks and rabbits are often kept for the sheer pleasure they give to children, while cows and horses of course serve more practical purposes. Both the latter need stabling in cold or wet weather. Rabbits should have a secure and sheltered hutch; ducks and geese a fairly good-sized pond, ideally with a natural flow of water running through it.

RIGHT   *A gaggle of geese go home to a safely fenced enclosure, complete with pond and shelter.*

OPPOSITE
ABOVE LEFT   *Kennels raised from the ground to keep them dry in wet weather.*

ABOVE RIGHT   *A row of wooden kennels accommodate three canine friends.*

BELOW LEFT   *Rabbits, ducks and chickens co-habit quite happily in a well organised Farmhouse garden.*

BELOW RIGHT   *Rabbits are contained in a hutch while tortoises of varying sizes wander freely around a fenced-in area of the garden.*

KEEPING BIRDS AND BEES

These are a joy in the garden, and most of us like to encourage them, but if yours is a truly Cottage-style or Farmhouse property (see Part One) you might well want to make special arrangements for them – to install an aviary and a few beehives.

Although you do not have to be an expert to keep birds, some knowledge is essential. Moreover, the particular species of bird will determine the size and kind of enclosure or cage needed. If you have the space, incorporate a tree (even a dead trunk and branches is better than nothing at all), bushes and a small pond or hollow stone for water. These will not only make your birds feel happier, but will greatly enhance the area's looks as well.

Since an aviary is so very obviously a man-made structure for wild creatures, plant around it so that it blends more naturally with its surround.

Bee-keeping is a more demanding activity, and one which few people nowadays are willing to undertake. Among the prerequisites are thorough knowledge, specialized equipment and a garden large enough to accommodate the hives some distance from the general outdoor living area (in a spot which will ensure that the flight path of the bees does not interfere with people using the garden). In some contemporary Cottage-style gardens, though, traditional white hives – albeit empty ones – are included simply for the effect!

RIGHT A *bird-table and bird-bath attract garden birds.*

OPPOSITE
ABOVE LEFT *An attractive and practical wooden bird-table.*

ABOVE RIGHT *Bird-cages are suspended from a pergola.*

BELOW LEFT *A pond adds charm to an aviary.*

BELOW RIGHT *Bird-cages hang in their own wooden shelter.*

If you are daunted by the idea of a hive, there is still, as we have mentioned, something special about a garden graced by bees and butterflies. Certain flowers and herbs (fennel, borage, lemon balm, thyme, mint and marjoram, for instance) will encourage these creatures, and by establishing the relevant plants close to the kitchen window you will be able to see and enjoy them as they buzz and flutter about.

Bees convert nectar into honey, but they also store pollen for food and thus help pollinate garden plants and flowers. Butterflies, on the other hand, are interested only in nectar.

One plant that is quick growing and particularly attractive to the latter, is the butterfly bush, *Buddleia davidii*, with its scented flower spikes. Others include the perennial *Sedum spectabile*, delphiniums (especially D. *grandiflorum*), anemones, crown daisies (*Chrysanthemum coronarium*) and the wonderfully sweet-smelling tuberose (*Polianthes tuberosa*), most of which will attract bees as well.

Among the trees and shrubs that attract both butterflies and bees are ericas (heather), jasmine, wisteria, several herbs including mints, thymes and marjoram, and in warm climates, bougainvillea.

A *medicinal herb garden planted with Jerusalem sage, wilde als (wild wormwood, a disinfecting herb used for coughs and colds), wormwood (a useful insecticide), motherwort (a tonic herb) and lady's bedstraw (traditionally used to cleanse the skin and to stuff mattresses and pillows).*

OPPOSITE *A well-organised kitchen garden with established artichokes on one side and rows of vegetables, including lettuce, carrots and spring onions, on the other.*

KITCHEN GARDENS

The popularity or otherwise of growing edible plants is linked directly to general economic prosperity: in times of plenty it wanes, and when budgets are pinched everybody, it seems, wants a kitchen garden. Certainly, as food prices continue to spiral, more and more people take to supplementing their shopping baskets from the garden, creating what the Americans call the 'edible landscape'.

Vegetable and herb gardens are fairly standard components of the modern residential property. The true kitchen garden, however, is distinctive: it incorporates both, and covers an entire area immediately outside the house. Traditional examples can be found in early American settler homes, where front gardens were planted with culinary herbs as well as flower species (roses, peonies, hollyhocks, poppies and marigolds); in English Cottage gardens of the 'chocolate-box' type, where every bit of ground available was planted, and brightly coloured flowers were displayed with gay abandon among edible plants; and of course in the famous French *potagers*, where decorative vegetables were arranged in attractive patterns in formal beds, usually hedged by fruit trees.

These arrangements were historically determined: the earliest gardens were utilitarian, planted with fruit, vegetables and herbs for the kitchen, and with herbs for medicinal use. By the 17th century separate herb gardens had made their appearance, so differentiating between purely decorative plants and those that had specific medicinal and culinary uses in the home. For instance, a book published in 1617 suggested that one section be planted in knots and squares with 'comely and durable' herbs and flowers, while another be designated for plants to be used in the kitchen.

Of course, the traditional kitchen garden was sizeable, usually divided by hard pathways into at least three sections so that plants could be rotated.

Most suburban properties are too small to accommodate the classical kitchen garden, but one can still adapt the principle to create an attractive mélange of the useful and the beautiful.

A HERB GARDEN

The earliest herb gardens were established in ancient times to provide plants not only for culinary use, but for medicines (sometimes grown in separate 'physic gardens'), and for perfumes. Some species were also grown for the protection they were believed to offer against evil forces.

Today most of us grow herbs for the kitchen, although, encouraged by authors such as Sarah Garland in England and Margaret Roberts in South Africa, there is a growing interest in plants that promote healthy living or have curative properties. Herbs may also be planted to create a focal point (in a tub perhaps), or used as ground cover, or as hedges and even for topiary (see pages 115-116).

The layout possibilities of the modern herb garden are endless. You could follow the example of the French parterre, or of the knot garden so popular in Tudor England; or establish a complex arrangement, such as those found in the grounds of monasteries, where herbs were cultivated for food, for healing and for religious ceremonies; or one in the tradition of a Cottage garden (see pages 33-35), with herbs mixed in with other plants; or simply plant a border alongside path, house or boundary fence.

A particularly successful design can be created with paving slabs placed on bare earth in a chequer-

board pattern. Here the concrete prevents invasive herb types from smothering the more delicate species and, at the same time, provides solid ground on which to walk on while tending and picking.

A wild herb meadow is another possibility, although, contrary to what one might expect, this requires careful planning and will take time to establish.

The wide selection of herbs available today includes shrubs such as rosemary, lemon verbena and lavender, which may be used to create a permanent framework; perennials that die back each year and then shoot again in spring; annuals, such as marjoram and basil, that need to be replanted on a seasonal basis, and even trees (the ever-popular bay, *Laurus nobilis*, for instance).

What you choose to plant will depend largely on the type of herb garden you have decided upon and the uses you have planned for the herbs. Since most culinary species have insignificant flowers, it would be advisable to include the ornamental and more aromatic herbs as well as those needed by the keen cook. Simply to crush the leaves of scented geraniums (*Pelargonium* spp.) in your fingers will give you pleasure, even if you do not intend using them for puddings; and lavender flowers will add colour whether or not you intend chopping them up for fruit salad. Likewise marigolds (*Calendula officinalis*) and nasturtiums (*Tropaeolum majus*), both of them edible and attractive species which also have remarkable medicinal qualities.

RIGHT   *Herbs make an attractive border.*

OPPOSITE
ABOVE LEFT   *Tiny tomatoes flourish in a herb garden.*

ABOVE RIGHT   *A wide variety of herbs are planted between concrete paving slabs and in pots.*

BELOW LEFT   *Marigolds and poppies brighten an informal herb garden packed with plants.*

BELOW RIGHT   *A wonderfully overgrown herb garden.*

THE VEGETABLE GARDEN

Nowadays, most people locate their vegetable gardens out of sight: accessibility to the kitchen is not as vital as for the herb garden, and position is a secondary consideration. Of more importance is that the ground is reasonably level, has good drainage and is fertile. Salad vegetables, in particular, need to be tender, and require not only good soil conditions but a also warm, sheltered spot.

Different vegetables need different minerals, and if you continue to grow the same type of plant in one spot year after year the relevant nutrients will simply be used up. Certain pests and diseases will also thrive and destroy the new plants. The answer is to rotate the crops. The suggestion here is that, to begin with – after enriching the soil with manure – you plant legumes (peas, and various beans), which will leave nitrogen in the ground, and leeks and onions (particularly those grown from seed), which will take advantage of the rich soil. Next season, plant nitrogen-loving leafy species, mainly of the Brassica family (broccoli, Brussels sprouts, cabbage, cauliflower and kohlrabi). In the third season it is the turn of the root vegetables – which, perhaps ironically, include two of the brassicas (turnips and swedes) as well as radishes and carrots (considered quick growing, or 'catch', crops). Various salad plants – lettuce, endive, rocket and low-growing garden cress – may be planted at the same time.

If you want to grow asparagus (a particulary time-consuming exercise), globe artichokes, rhubarb or soft fruits such as strawberries, it would be advisable to set aside a separate patch. Potatoes will probably need yet another area, simply because they take up so much space.

The layout of the vegetable garden will depend largely on the site chosen, the space you have available, and the plants you intend growing. If possible, divide it into several small but distinct patches to accommodate rotation planting.

The conventional vegetable garden is arranged in rows although, to conserve space, it may be necessary to plant in blocks. You can economize further by training climbing and trailing plants (cucumbers, marrows, tomatoes, beans and so on) up wire fences or wooden trelliswork.

Certain space-saving growing techniques may also be applied. Intercropping, for instance, will enable you to cultivate fast-growing plants – garden cress, endives or even radishes – beneath cabbages or lettuces, which take longer to establish themselves.

RIGHT   *A vegetable garden established in a planter alongside a boundary wall that shields the service area.*

OPPOSITE
ABOVE LEFT   *Tomatoes and lettuces flourish in a border reserved especially for salad plants.*

ABOVE RIGHT   *An attractive vegetable garden which has been laid out in traditional rows.*

BELOW LEFT   *Well-established Pride of India trees provide welcome shade in an informal vegetable garden.*

BELOW RIGHT   *A secluded strip of garden alongside the house has been reserved for vegetables.*

AN ORCHARD

Nowadays the fruit we buy in most shops is selectively cultivated and not at all like fruits you would grow yourself: invariably bigger and more prettily coloured, though often less succulent and tasty. The problem here is that relatively few people are able to set aside enough space to to meet their ongoing needs for fresh fruit. However, there are considerations apart from the purely practical: fruit trees, for instance, will add charm to any garden, especially when in blossom.

An orchard is an area, usually located at the bottom of the garden, where rows and rows of trees produce harvests of apples, plums, pears, apricots and so on. However, in centuries past, fruit trees were often trained into fans, or as espaliers (with long branches running horizontally along supports), or cordons with single stems, often at an angle to save space. Generally a tree shaped in this way will produce less fruit, but what it does yield is likely to be of a far better quality and greater size.

In the Cottage garden (see pages 33-35), fruit and nut trees were always in evidence, but not in the form of an orchard. Instead they were often planted as part of the hedgerow (in order to save space) and fruit bushes and perennials (raspberries and strawberries were a favourite) could be found in among the flowers and herbs.

Today, extensive orchards are more or less restricted to farmland, but it is still quite possible to establish a smaller, more versatile arrangement in a fairly limited area. Ideally, plant a selection of both summer and winter fruits that will ripen at different times throughout the year.

The specific fruit grown will of course depend on the climatic and soil conditions in your region. Early-flowering cultivars, including apricots, should be avoided in areas subject to late frosts and cold winds, while all fruit trees planted near the sea should be regularly hosed to get rid of salt.

RIGHT   *Apples litter the ground of a small domestic orchard established in a fairly limited area. Other fruits planted here include pears, peaches and lemons.*

OPPOSITE   *Where there is not much space, fruit trees may be combined with other plants. Here, a pomegranate tree, laden with rosy fruit, adds colour to the garden.*

A *man-made waterfall trickles into a splendid lily-pond; water-loving plants soften the rocky surfaces.*

OPPOSITE *An elaborate rockery and pond-graced water garden boasts a naturalistic waterfall that links it to a cool, blue plunge-pool.*

WATER IN THE GARDEN

Water is a cleansing, cooling and restful element, and it offers wonderful possibilities in a garden, whatever its size or style, its movement and sound evoking a variety of moods. A tranquil, reflective pond soothes; a lively little brook, trickling and splashing through plants, stones and rocks, catching the sunlight as it goes, invigorates the spirit.

Just as the garden as a whole can be formal or informal in character, so too can the water garden and the swimming pool or spa area. In the formal category are swimming pools and ponds of a regular, geometric shape, as well as most precast fountain arrangements; in the latter are irregularly shaped, natural-looking ponds, streams, waterfalls and so on.

The informal pond (or swimming pool), therefore, will generally blend with its surrounds, whereas the formal variety will stand out as an attractive, albeit obviously artificial, feature. But whatever the design – formal, natural or purely whimsical – a well-planned water garden will add a very special quality to the outdoor area.

Water has been a feature of the domestic garden since the earliest recorded times. In ancient Egypt, a central pool was often the focus (large estate gardens, indeed, incorporated many pools, though these were designed as much for irrigation as for effect). The grand villa gardens of classical Rome were laid out with fountains and canal-like stretches of water. Centuries later, during the Renaissance, formal water gardens yet again flourished in Italy. Eighteenth-century English landscape gardens, many designed by the celebrated Capability Brown (see page 202), were graced by vast naturalistic lakes.

But it is the Japanese who have excelled, developing the use of water into the most delicate of art forms, giving meaning to even the tiniest trickle of water. A Japanese gardener will create, for example, a pleasing little composition from hollowed-out stones with bamboo fountains spilling into them; or lead rainwater to flow into a stone basin. Where there is no water, an arrangement of stones may suggest a stream; raked gravel the sea.

PONDS AND STREAMS

A pond can transform even the dullest and most ordinary of areas. And here the choice, once again, lies between the formal and the informal, the decision determined by the effect you want to achieve, by the site possibilities, and to a degree by the overall style of your garden.

Formal ponds and pools are usually circular or rigidly geometric (and may even be raised off the ground), and reflective in effect, introducing a gentle, soothing element to garden, courtyard or patio.

A natural pond is often fed by a stream, and will usually lie at a low point in the garden. Logically, therefore, a man-made pond of this kind should be similarly sited – perhaps in a well-shaded 'dead' area. The addition of rocks and boulders to conceal the edges of the pool, and of marsh- and tropical-type plants, will enhance the natural look.

An artificial stream must also appear natural, with perhaps small rockeries for waterfalls and cascades along its course (though electric pumps will be needed to recirculate the water and ensure a constant flow). The surrounds, too, must also look as if they are part of the landscape. If there is no stream to feed the pond, then water will have to be constantly topped up and peripheral plants (especially bog-loving species) regularly watered.

RIGHT   A *rocky pond spills across a driveway.*

OPPOSITE
ABOVE LEFT   An *attractive fish-pond established in the corner of a courtyard. Design: Errol Cooper.*

ABOVE RIGHT   *Ponds nestle against a boundary wall.*

BELOW LEFT   An *attractive garden planted to accommodate a natural stream.*

BELOW RIGHT   A *water feature with streams and ponds.*

Ponds and pools may be constructed of brick or concrete; dug into the earth and lined with plastic or vinyl; or a ready-made container (most commonly fibreglass or fibrecement) may be sunk into the ground. A traditional technique in the United Kingdom is clay puddling, where a suitable clay or chalk is moulded and worked to create a 150-mm (6-inch) thick 'waterproof' lining.

Consider whether to stock your pond with fish and, if so, of what type. While goldfish ponds are popular, more and more people today are opting for koi (Japanese carp). Although goldfish will thrive in quite shallow water, a koi pond should be at least 600 mm (2 ft) deep, though there should, ideally, be a range of depths so that these fish can move between the cooler deep and warmer shallow water. While *all* fish ponds need plants to oxygenate the water and to provide the fish material to spawn and nibble on, a koi pond should also be filtered to keep the water clear.

Some plants are of course better adapted than others to live in water or at the water's edge. Day lilies and irises will thrive on the brink of a pond, while water hyacinths, and, of course, the all-time favourite water-lily will grow in the water itself. Arum lilies will grow in marshy soil or in shallow water.

If yours is a reflective pond, do not allow it to become overgrown with aquatic plants. Attractive as this may be, many species grow very quickly and will soon obscure all reflection.

FOUNTAINS

It has been said that fountains are to formal pools what streams are to informal ponds. Certainly each introduces sound and movement to the garden. Fountains are also a form of 'living sculpture', exploiting the interaction of light and water, creating impressions ranging from the splendid to the whimsical. And a fountain, set perhaps in a small pool, will enable you to introduce the element of water into even the smallest outdoor space.

The type of fountain you choose will, of course, depend on the water feature it is to embellish. There are many options, each of which will produce its own effect – and each requires a pump to enable it to operate. A simple spray jet will spurt high into the air, arcing as it falls, while other mechanisms will create a more constant pattern or dome of water.

The simplest kind of spout will allow water to overflow – perhaps through a gargoyle – into a catching pool or bowl below; while a more elaborate fountain may incorporate a contemporary sculpture of some kind. One of the most popular types is that which has three tiers, usually made of precast concrete, in the classical style but also, sometimes, handmade in ceramics. A series of round bowls may also be placed to form a tiered feature. A bubble fountain, which disturbs the surface of the water, will produce sound as well as movement.

Though they are subject to the whims of fashion, fountains have been used for centuries. They were, for instance, an essential element in the inner courtyards of ancient societies, and often served as a focal point in Medieval gardens. The most famous and elaborate designs – those created in the 16th and 17th centuries – are to be found in various parts of Europe, and include the spectacular waterworks at Cardinal Ippolito d'Este's villa in Tivoli, Italy, where the Pathway of the One Hundred Fountains is still a celebrated landmark; the prankish water jets concealed in a courtyard at the Villa Lante, Cardinal Gambara's country retreat near Bagnaia (also in Italy); the outrageous hydraulics at King Louis XIV's Palace of Versailles, where mills and pumps fed by water from the River Seine operated 1400 fountains in a magnificent garden designed by Le Nôtre (see page 204); and the preposterously prankish water arrangements devised at Schloss Hellbrunn, Austria (the place was built as an archbishop's residence). Here, an ingenious system using natural water pressure to operate fountains and 'water games', would squirt guests with sudden jets as they sat around a table in the central courtyard.

RIGHT   *A tiered pond with precast fountain in the upper level.*

OPPOSITE
ABOVE LEFT   *A simple but formal fountain in the parterre garden at Tuynhuys in Cape Town, South Africa.*

ABOVE RIGHT   *Standard roses around a fountain.*

BELOW LEFT   *A charming feature in a courtyard.*

BELOW RIGHT   *A simple spurting fountain in a niche.*

SWIMMING POOLS

The decision to build a swimming pool is usually related to leisure-time needs rather than the desire simply to include water in the garden. Similarly, the visual effect of most pools is of course quite different to that of fish- and lily-ponds, as they tend to dominate, if not the entire garden, certainly the section where they are located.

Thus it is very important to site a swimming pool carefully. If you value an indoor-outdoor lifestyle, the pool is best positioned close to the house, preferably adjacent to an existing patio (see pages 137-147) or where one can easily be built. On the other hand, should you decide on a summerhouse or gazebo, or a detached outdoor entertainment area with built-in cooking facilities complete with seating and so on, this will probably be a more sensible location. Either way, though, try to screen the pool area so that it is not seen from every other part of the garden.

Fountains, rockeries and waterfalls may be included in the pool design and water reticulation system. Similarly, the swimming pool may be successfully incorporated into a water garden with ponds and other features. Although the two elements cannot be directly connected (aquatic plants and fish do not like the chlorine and other chemicals essential for pool hygiene), they may be linked visually, in which event the pool style chosen should be in keeping with the ornamention. Ensure that harmony is retained in the plantings, or by uniting disparate elements in some other way – for instance, with a rockery that encloses the informal pond and borders the pool on one or more sides.

Choice of pool type will be determined by a number of factors, including of course preferred style and price. Moreover, you will probably have a preference in terms of the construction method. But the wide choice will enable you to build something that blends with and enhances the garden, whatever its character. A traditionally blue, geometrically shaped pool, for example, will fit the formal plan, while a beach pool or one with a charcoal or brown finish will harmonize with the more casual approach.

RIGHT   *The swimming pool at Villa Chiamar, one of the estates of late Italian multi-millionaire Mario Chiavelli.*

OPPOSITE
ABOVE LEFT   *A unique brick paved swimming pool built more than 20 years ago by architect Gerald Gordon.*

ABOVE RIGHT   *A circular swimming pool contrasts with the angular lines of an ultra-modern house designed by architect Carmel Back.*

BELOW LEFT   *A seaside pool with charcoal finish.*

BELOW RIGHT   *Facebrick retaining walls, a railway sleeper and paved surround lend form to a newly landscaped garden.*

HOT WATER SPAS

Artificially heated spas have gained in popularity in recent years, largely because of their therapeutic potential: a spa will improve blood circulation and, as air and water jets massage tired muscles, help the body to relax and rejuvenate.

Although often housed under cover, a spa may just as easily be built in the garden, alongside a swimming pool, or on a patio leading from the house. The siting decision will be determined by function: if health is a major factor, you may prefer to maintain privacy, but if you intend inviting friends to share its pleasures you will need to locate it in a spot easily accessible to all.

The most common type of hot-water spa is moulded acrylic, available in a number of shapes, sizes and colours. These usually incorporate some form of seating, perhaps with a contoured recliner; the more expensive designs may include a rimflow feature that allows water to flow over the edge of the spa into a channel.

While acrylic spas are generally sunk into the ground, a wooden tub is more often positioned above the surface. The latter, American in origin, are often made of redwood, although other woods (oak, cedar and teak) are used in some countries.

Some pool manufacturers will build concrete spas: a sensible option if it is to be sited alongside a pool or, perhaps, incorporated in the pool design. It is important, in this instance, to ensure that all jets are properly sealed to prevent any risk of leakage.

All spas have their own pump systems, usually with a cartridge filter, and are heated up to 40 °C (104 °F). In spa pools – unlike smaller spa baths that are usually installed in the bathroom and refilled, emptied and cleaned every time they are used – the hot water is retained and chlorinated to keep it clear and hygienic. To prevent temperature loss, an insulation blanket is laid over the surface of the water when it is not in use. Some companies will also supply a timber lid (or you can have one custom-made) that looks more attractive and serves as an added safety precaution – a valuable supplementary feature if you have young children.

OPPOSITE *A circular hot water spa nestles between man-made rocks and lush foliage.*

RIGHT *Planters packed with marigolds and pots filled with impatiens are a colourful backdrop for a hot water spa.*

A *trampoline, set into the ground alongside a swimming pool, is a perfect place for adults to exercise and for older children to play.*

OPPOSITE   A *private putting green is an ideal playground for the keen golfer. The grass is fine-leafed and hard-wearing, and quite unlike the adjoining lawn.*

PLACES FOR SPORT AND PLAY

Unlike many adults, children do not need complex and sophisticated play equipment to keep them happy: they will improvize, adapt whatever is at hand. Given a well planned and pretty garden, they will find nooks and crannies that provide venues for wonderfully inventive games. By the same token, if you take the time and trouble to create a play area especially for them, you are more likely to avoid broken shrubs and footprints in the flower beds.

While facilities for adults (tennis court, croquet lawn, putting green and so on) are geared for specific activities, an area suitable for a young child will simply provide a safe and interesting place in which to play; that for an older child on the other hand should, ideally, stimulate a sense of adventure.

Age will determine not only what is to be provided, but also where the play area should be sited. For small children, it will need to be located near the house to enable you to keep an eye on them, but the older they get the more independent they become, preferring to play out of sight.

If yours is a new garden, you will have the opportunity to plan from scratch and, if you cannot afford to incorporate everything immediately, you will at least be able to look ahead, and ensure that the layout will be able to accommodate specific outdoor areas – tennis court, Wendy house, swimming pool or spa – at a later stage.

An established garden may on the other hand force you to make major changes, or perhaps to compromise. For instance, the only level space large enough to take a tennis court may be occupied by the vegetable patch or herb garden, or the only area suitable for the planned children's adventure playground may be directly outside the living room. Having decided that you want a tennis court *and* a vegetable garden, you will have to re-locate and re-establish the latter, which can take several years; and having set your heart on the playground, you will either have to put up with the inevitable noise or find another site, even if it means cutting down trees and digging out established plants which may not survive transplanting.

THE PLAYGROUND

Children's likes, dislikes, needs and wants change as frequently as the seasons, but, still, you would like them to get as much pleasure from the garden as you do. Options range from a simple lawned and level patch for ball games to a secluded area or secret garden where they can grow their own fruit, vegetables and flowers.

Age of course is the major determinant. A toddler should not be left in the garden unattended, although if you can enclose and secure an area next to the house, you may be able to leave a door open, and keep a watchful eye from the kitchen or living room while he or she plays.

A great favourite at this age is the sand pit, which can be quickly, easily and inexpensively prepared, either below or above ground. Ready-made containers and tractor tyres are probably the simplest ingredients. In the latter instance the inner tube is removed and the outer rubber left to retain sand. An inexpensive alternative is to use planed timber or logs to form a box, either pre-assembled or knocked together *in situ*. Or, thirdly, the basic structure may be built of brick to provide a permanent feature.

RIGHT *Colourful playground equipment includes a jungle gym with slide, and swings made from old tyres.*

OPPOSITE
ABOVE LEFT *This corner of the garden has been set aside for playground equipment.*

ABOVE RIGHT *An elaborate tree-house provides an intriguing setting for play.*

BELOW LEFT *A garden Wendy house provides a storage place for toys, as well as a place to play.*

BELOW RIGHT *A mini adventure playground established on the slopes of a mountainside garden.*

Use clean building sand or dune sand as the filling. Beach sand is also an option, provided of course it is not polluted. Cover the sandpit when not in use to prevent animals (especially cats) soiling the contents.

Small children also love swings and slides, jungle-gyms and see-saws. A variety of factory-manufactured designs are available, though if you are handy you could make your own. A jungle-gym with a flat play-platform is reasonably simple to construct from treated poles and planks. A swing – with either a solid timber or tyre seat – may be suspended from the structure or from the branch of a sturdy tree.

Water play is also popular, but for safety's sake use a portable pool that can be emptied when not in use. Moulded plastic, blow-up plastic and vinyl pools, set on a framework, are all widely available.

As the child gets older, he or she will want to explore, to seek not only wider spaces but also nooks and crannies which stimulate creative free play. Once they start climbing (and are able to do so safely), tree houses and rope ladders will provide great sources of amusement. A strong rope flung over the equally tough branch of an established tree will cost very little, but is guaranteed to provide endless hours of pleasure.

Little girls love Wendy houses. Ensure, though, that yours is large enough for use in later years, perhaps as a hideaway, den or perhaps as a tool shed.

All children, regardless of age, are fond of pretty things, and it is a delightful idea for them to plant their own secret garden with flowers they can pick – and with vegetables they can eat.

ADULT RECREATION

Relatively few modern properties are large enough to accommodate more than a swimming pool (see pages 191-192) and perhaps a practice net for basketball or netball. But if you have the space and a suitable site, other options include a tennis court, croquet lawn, putting green or even a bowling green (which may of course be much narrower than the orthodox green, but must, if it is to serve its purpose, extend to the full length).

Although not strictly a part of the garden plan, a squash court may also be included in the scheme. This will either be constructed as part of the house, or as an outbuilding, perhaps with access to a sauna, spa or swimming pool.

A tennis court requires a level area of at least 650 sq m (7 000 sq ft), 36 m x 18 m (118 ft x 59 ft) in size. A half-court (offered by some companies) is another option, though here you will have to use a different kind of racquet and a softer ball.

Space permitting, a tennis court – which is not the most visually attractive of features – is best sited well away from the house, and positioned so that it lies from north to south (rather than from east to west) to provide the most practical arrangement in terms of sunlight and shadow. It would be preferable, too, that it is not shaded by tall trees – which means, of course, that its high wire fence (green mesh is the most suitable and most common) will be very open to view. To soften the effect, you could plant a low ornamental hedge (of rosemary, perhaps, or lavender) or depending on your garden style, establish an informal mixed border of low flowering shrubs and perennial plants.

A games lawn – for bowls, croquet and so on – must be hardy and absolutely flat. Certain grasses, fine-leafed and hard-wearing, are more suitable for this purpose than others. They include Florida (*Cynodon transvaalensis*); Royal Cape (*Cynodon dactylon var.*); and Magennis (*Cynodon dactylon 'Magennisii'*).

OPPOSITE   A *hardy front lawn makes an interesting croquet course. Ideally the area should be absolutely flat.*

RIGHT   A *row of standard roses and a neatly trimmed lavender hedge planted alongside a tennis court.*

GLOSSARY

Alpine Strictly speaking a plant which is indigenous to the mountains. Nowadays the term is often used for any plant suitable for rock gardens and rockeries.

Annual Any plant which completes its life cycle in a maximum of a year. Generally planted in spring and removed in autumn, or when it dies in winter.

Aquatic Plant which grows in, or partially submerged in, the water. Aquatics are essential for oxygenating the water.

Arboretum A sizeable tree collection or botanical tree garden.

Arbour Small-scale garden shelter, often covered with climbing plants.

Asphalt A homogenous mixture of bitumen, aggregate and proprietary filler mostly used hot to 'tar' various surfaces including driveways.

Avenue An approach lined with trees.

Baker, Sir Herbert (1862-1946) British architect who spent two decades working in South Africa where he designed hundreds of houses and complementary garden structures.

Balustrade A fence, traditionally of stone, consisting of a rail or coping on a row of balusters or pillars. Typically used in classical Italian gardens or to edge a terrace.

Bed Area of ground used for planting. Strictly speaking a bed is found in the centre of a garden as opposed to a border which is round the edge. (See *Bloom, Alan*)

Bedding plants Annuals or bienneals planted for display in a single season.

Bell glass A large bell-shaped jar or cloche which was developed in France to protect early crops. Seldom used nowadays.

Belvedere A raised summer house or turret, traditionally Italian in style.

Biennial Plant which completes its life-cycle in two growing seasons; forming a green, leafy plant in the first, then flowering and seeding before it dies in the second.

Bloom, Alan (born 1906) British nurseryman and author who specializes in herbaceous perennials and alpines. Displays his enormous plant collection in island beds which he popularized.

Bog plant That which thrives in marshy conditions.

Bonsai A Japanese art which trains trees to look mature and natural in a miniature state.

Border Flowerbed around the edge of a garden.

Border plants Term synonymous with herbaceous (or hardy) perennials.

Botanic garden Place where plants are grown for botanical, rather than horticultural, interest. Traditionally plants will be grouped in families, rather than according to appearance and effect.

Brookes, John (born 1933) Influential garden designer and author of a number of successful gardening books.

Brown, Lancelot (Capability) (1716-1783) Gardener who earned his nickname because he believed all gardens had 'capabilities'. Loathed formal gardens which he replaced en masse with vast natural landscapes at many of the great English country houses, including Blenheim Palace. Although condemned by many for this approach, his vision of English parkland is now generally accepted.

Canal Stretch of water frequently found in classical gardens. Not usually navigable.

Cane Raspberries, strawberries and other plants with similar stem.

Carpet bedding Popular Victorian style of planting where small plants are tightly packed to form mosaic or carpet-like patterns. Seldom seen in contemporary gardens.

Cascade Waterfall which runs down a stepped slope; or a series of small waterfalls. Popular in classical Italian and French gardens.

Catch crop Vegetable that matures quickly, carrots and radishes for example.

Chambers, Sir William (1723-1796) Influential architect who is thought to have been the first designer to suggest massing flowers according to colour. Strong critic of 'Capability' Brown.

Chinoserie Design in the Chinese style (particularly 18th century), with brightly coloured fretwork, pavilions and bridges.

Clay puddling Traditional technique used to seal the sides and base of large, natural ponds.

Climber Plant which has the ability to climb.

Cloche Although this word means 'a bell' and was used to describe the original French 'bell glass' (see previous page), it is now used to describe protective structures of other sorts, including miniature flat-sided greenhouses designed to cover rows of vegetables.

Conifer Any cone-bearing tree (e.g. pine, fir). Also includes yews and juniper trees which have fleshy fruits. Most are evergreen with needles or thin strap-shaped leaves.

Conservatory A greenhouse usually attached to the house and utilized as much by people as plants. (See also *Cloche*)

Cordon A tree or plant severely pruned to a single stem. May be grown obliquely.

Deciduous Plant which sheds its leaves, usually during the autumn season.

Dot plant Taller plant found dotted about in amongst short plants; especially in carpet beds of the Victorian type.

Espalier Tree – especially apple and pear – trained on a latticework of wire or wood. Branches are usually selected and encouraged to grow in a particular shape, usually horizontally.

Evergreen Plant that does not lose all its leaves in the winter months.

Exotic Plant introduced from another country.

Family Any group of plant genera sharing a set of basic characteristics; flower or leaf composition, for instance.

Fern Non-flowering plant that reproduces by means of spores found on the underside of leaf-like fronds.

Fibrecement Material composed of cement and a variety of organic fibres that is used to make certain building materials.

Foliage plant Plant grown for its leaves rather than for flowers or fruit.

Folly Fanciful construction built for appearance rather than practical use. Common in the 17th century; often inspired by the ruins of ancient Greece and Rome.

Garland, Sarah (born 1944) Contemporary British author of several popular books on herbs, spices and wild flowers.

Gazebo Pavilion or raised turret on a house with a view; or small building located at the end of a raised terrace.

Genus (pl. genera) Group of plants with common characteristics. A genus may comprise one or more species; and if several genera have a common ancestor, they are grouped together as a plant family.

Gnomon The triangular plate of a sundial.

Greenhouse Glass structure used to protect plants from the weather.

Grotto Natural or, more usually, artificial cave in a garden. Common in classical Italian gardens.

Ground cover Wide range of plants which will form a blanket over the soil.

Guild, Trisha Internationally renowned British interior designer, whose fabric and wallpaper ranges are marketed world-wide. Author of several books on décor and gardens.

Herb Any non-woody, non-shrubby annual, biennial or perennial plant. Term also used to describe wide range of aromatic plants.

Herbaceous Any perennial herb (with soft or sappy rather than woody growth) that dies back to ground level in autumn or winter. Herbaceous borders are customarily filled with these plants.

Hybrid Plant produced by cross breeding two species or genera. Often denoted with a multiplication sign (e.g. Abelia x grandiflora) between two plant names.

In situ Term used to describe something still in its original place. Concrete may be cast *in situ*, seeds planted *in situ* or a rock left to form a seat *in situ*.

Island beds Style of planting popularized by British nurseryman Alan Bloom where irregular, curving beds are created in a lawn.

Jekyll, Gertrude (1843-1932) Gifted artist who turned to garden design and writing because of failing eyesight – and produced many influential books on garden design. She subsequently worked with architect Edwin Luytens, and became one of the most influential designers of this century.

Johnston, Lawrence (died 1958) American expatriate who developed the now famous gardens at Hidcote Manor in England.

Kitchen garden That part of the garden where vegetables, herbs and flowers are planted for the house. The French kitchen gardens or *jardins potagers* were formal and established on small plots.

Knot Formal, ornamental flowerbed created with a twisted, decorative design in Tudor England.

Landscape (Landskip) Movement Revolutionary garden design which began in England during the 18th century and led to the destruction of many fine, old gardens.

Laterite Mixture of fine gravel and ferruginous clay; watered and rolled to form a smooth surface. Particularly well suited to walkways and paths.

Le Nôtre, André (1613-1700) Great French garden designer who worked on a lavish scale. Best known for his work at Versailles. Many Le Nôtre gardens outside France are, in fact, creations by pupils and imitators.

Loudon, John Claudius (1783-1843) Well-known British gardener and son of a Scottish farmer who produced books, magazines and an encyclopedia of gardening aimed at the wealthy middle-classes. He introduced the terms 'picturesque' and later, 'gardenesque' landscaping.

Loggia Gallery open to the air on one or both sides. Originally designed as a shady walk in Italian gardens.

Lutyens, Sir Edwin (1869-1944) English architect who collaborated with Gertrude Jekyll on many garden projects. A vehement opponent of the Modern Movement in architecture.

Malthoid Bituminous felt used to waterproof roofs of sheds, dog kennels and so forth.

Marsh Land that is permanently waterlogged.

Micro-climate Climate of a localized area, often within a single garden.

Morris, William (1834-1896) Victorian artist, designer, writer and poet. Leading figure in the 19th-century Arts and Crafts Movement which resulted in the formation of various guilds and craft societies. He favoured a simple, romantic garden style with rural traditions and loathed carpet bedding.

Moss Non-flowering, single cell plant which retains water.

Nicolson, Sir Harold (1886-1968) Husband of Vita Sackville-West (Lady Victoria Nicolson). Together they created the famous gardens at Sissinghurst.

Parterre Ornamental flowerbed created low on the ground and intended to be viewed from above. Very popular in France during the late 16th and early 17th centuries.

Patio Any open-air living area.

Pavilion Light, ornamental structure.

Paxton, Sir Joseph (1803-1865) Horticulturalist and engineer who popularized the greenhouse in Victorian England. Best know for his awesome Crystal Palace, designed for the Great Exhibition of 1851.

Perennial A plant which lives and flowers for more than two years. The growth (primarily leaves) of many perennials dies down in winter and then revives in spring. Generally herbaceous rather than with woody stems. Has roots which will survive for many years.

Pergola Structure of pillars and cross beams usually planted with climbers. Often built over patios and carports.

Pleaching Traditional technique used to form a dense hedge by interweaving branches of plants until they can be clipped. Lower trunk or stem is often stripped bare.

Potager Classic French kitchen garden.

Rambler Rose or other plant with long but droopy stems. Needs to be supported.

Repton, Humphry (1752-1818) Successor of 'Capability' Brown in the Landscape Movement. Less dogmatic and happy to allow terraces and flowers back into the foreground of gardens.

Roberts, Margaret (born 1937) Contemporary South African author whose books and television features on herbs have earned her great recognition on the subject.

Robinson, William (1838-1935) Famous gardening journalist and author who became foreman at the Royal Botanic Society's gardens in Regent's Park, London. Started *The Garden* magazine and subsequently met Gertrude Jekyll, who became a contributor. He loathed formal gardens, especially carpet bedding.

Sackville-West, Vita (Victoria) (1892-1962) British poet, novelist and gardening journalist whose garden at Sissinghurst in Kent is internationally renowned.

Shadecloth Protective woven covering.

Shrub Plant with a woody stem.

Species Group of plants sharing distinctive characteristics; each with a two-word Latin name.

Stoep Verandah at front, and sometimes the side, of house; in particular, that built in Cape Dutch style.

Succulent Plant with fleshy leaves and stem with juice or sap.

Terracotta Baked earth of a brownish-red colour, used to make pots, tiles and so on.

Topiary Method of cutting trees and bushes into ornamental shapes. First known in Roman times, and then during the Middle Ages. Particularly popular during both the 17th and 19th centuries.

Treillage Trelliswork used as a screen, to add height to a wall, or to create a trompe l'oeil effect in the garden. Sometimes used to create elaborate archtectural features.

Trompe l'oeil Picture or device of some kind which is designed to 'deceive the eye'. Although paint is a frequent medium, in gardens the effect is more usually achieved with treillage.

Werf Yard, particularly of Cape Dutch homestead.

FURTHER READING

Bander, Robert (editor), *Color (sic) in Your Garden*, Sunset Books, Menlo Park, California, 1975.

Brookes, John, *The Small Garden*, Marshall Cavendish, London, 1977; *The Garden Book*, Dorling Kindersley, London, 1984.

Conran, Terence, *New House Book*, Conran Octopus, London, 1985.

Eliovson, Sima, *Gardening the Japanese Way*, Howard Timmins, Cape Town, 1970; *Garden Design for Southern Africa*, Macmillan, Johannesburg, 1983.

Evans, Hazel, *The Patio Garden*, Frances Lincoln, London, 1985.

Fourie, Hester, *The South African Garden Designer*, Tafelberg, Cape Town, 1984.

Gardiner, Nancy, *Beautiful Gardens of South Africa*, Struik Timmins, Cape Town, 1991.

Garland, Sarah, *The Herb Garden*, Frances Lincoln, London, 1984.

Gilbert, Zoe and Hadfield, Jack, *Down-to-Earth Fruit and Vegetable Gardening in South Africa*, Struikhof, 1987.

Gilbert, Zoe, *Gardening in South Africa*, C. Struik, Cape Town, 1983; *Rose Growing in South Africa*, C. Struik, Cape Town, 1984.

Godbold-Simpson, *Small Gardens: a South African Guide*, C. Struik, Cape Town, 1987.

Innes, Jocaste, *Exterior Detail*, Collins and Brown, London, 1990.

Jansen, Chris, *50 Cape Dutch Houses*, Don Nelson Publishers, Cape Town, 1981.

Johnson, Hugh, *The Principles of Gardening*, Mitchell Beazley, London, 1980.

Joyce, David (General Editor), *Garden Styles: An Illustrated History of Design and Tradition*, Pyramid Books, London, 1989.

Joyce, Peter and Hartdegen, Jacqueline and Paddy,

The Complete Book of Home Planning in South Africa, C. Struik, Cape Town, 1986.

Keen, Mary, *The Glory of the English Garden*, Barrie and Jenkins, London, 1989.

Kench, John, *Cape Dutch Homesteads*, C. Struik, Cape Town, 1981.

Larkcom, Joy, *The Salad Garden*, Frances Lincoln, London, 1984.

Latymer, Hugo, *The Mediterranean Gardener*, Frances Lincoln, London, 1990.

Libraire Larousse/Mon Jardin Ma Maison, *Larousse Gardening and Gardens* (English translation), Paul Hamlyn, London, 1990.

Longley, Susanna, *Design a Garden with Trisha Guild*, Viking, London, 1989.

Loxton, Howard (editor), *The Garden*, Bok Books International, Manzini and Durban, 1991.

Lloyd, Christopher and Bird, Richard, *The Cottage Garden*, Dorling Kindersley, London, 1990.

McGowan, John and DuBern, Roger, *The Book of Home Restoration*, Ebury Press, London, 1985.

Mozley, Teresa, *Everyday Gardening*, Ward Lock, London, 1977.

Paul, Anthony and Rees, Yvonne, *The Water Garden*, Frances Lincoln, London, 1986.

Pienaar, Kristo, *The South African What Flower is That?*, C. Struik, Cape Town, 1984; *Grow South African Plants*, C. Struik, Cape Town, 1985.

Reader's Digest Association, *Illustrated Encyclopaedia of Gardening in South Africa*, Reader's Digest, Cape Town, 1984.

Reid, Owen A., *Gardening for the Vase*, Jonathan Ball/Human & Rousseau, South Africa, 1987.

Reid, Owen A. and Kirsten, Keith, *Patios for South Africa*, Human & Rousseau, Cape Town, 1990.

Roberts, Margaret, *Cook with Herbs and Spices*,

Southern Book Publishers, Johannesburg, 1988.

Rose, Graham, *The Low Maintenance Garden*, Frances Lincoln, London, 1983; *The Traditional Garden Book*, Dorling Kindersley, London, 1989.

Sheat, W.G., *The A-Z of Gardening in South Africa*, C. Struik, Cape Town, 1982.

Simpson, Murray (editor), *Annuals for the South African Garden*, Centaur, Cape Town, 1984.

Stevens, David, *Pergolas, Arbours, Gazebos, Follies*, Ward Lock, London, 1987.

Stevenson, Violet, *The Wild Garden*, Frances Lincoln, London, 1985.

Struik Group, The, *Wild Flowers of South Africa*, C. Struik, Cape Town, 1980.

Swift, Penny, *Build Your Own Braai*, C. Struik, Cape Town, 1987; *Build Your Own Carport*, C. Struik, Cape Town, 1988; *The Complete South African House Book*, Struik Timmins, Cape Town, 1991; *Swimming Pools and Spas for South African Homes*, Southern Book Publishers, Halfway House, 1992; *Step-by-Step Outdoor Brickwork*, Struik Timmins, Cape Town, 1992.

Swift, Penny and Goodbrand, Vaughn, *The Complete Book of Owner Building in South Africa*, Struik Publishers, Cape Town, 1992.

Taylor, Jane, *The Romantic English Garden*, Victoria's Secret and George Weidenfield and Nicolson, London, 1990.

Toogood, Alan, *Secret Gardens*, Ward Lock, London, 1987.

Wemyss, Diana, *The South African Book of Garden Ideas*, Struik Publishers, Cape Town, 1988.

Williams, Robin, *The Garden Planner*, Frances Lincoln, London, 1990.

Wilson, Andrew, *Garden Style Source Book*, Headline Book Publishing, London, 1989.

INDEX